Praise for *Great Fundraising Organizations*

"A very simple idea morphed into a 10-year program of research, the most exciting scientific project I have ever been involved with, and the generation of literally billions of dollars for nonprofits around the globe."

—Professor Adrian Sargeant,
Institute for Sustainable Philanthropy

"Being part of this journey has been a privilege – I wholeheartedly endorse Great Fundraising the book, the training, and the people at Revolutionise International Ltd. This has underpinned my approach to building teams, engaging donors, and influencing my organisations to achieve growth every year for the last 10 years."

—Jayne George,
Director of Fundraising, Marketing and Media, the RNLI, UK

"Unrestricted income means sustainability, independence, and innovation for any INGO. At Lutheran World Relief, we have practically doubled our unrestricted revenue in five years since implementing the Great Fundraising programme that this book lays out so clearly. We now have an organisation which is united behind our vibrant fundraising culture."

Vice President for External Relations,
Lutheran World Relief, USA

"There are many good ideas but there are a few great ideas. The challenge is to know the difference. And with fundraising, it is Great Fundraising that propels your organisation towards enabling the great ideas to happen. The Royal Flying Doctor Service of Australia is a great organisation with great services underpinned by great fundraising thanks to the principles and practices in this book. We at RFDS have grown our service capacity exponentially by placing the "business of fundraising" at the core of organizational survival and growth. There is no mission if there is no money, and this book enables the board and staff to achieve the ambitions every organization has for the people it serves."

—Scott Chapman,
CEO, Royal Flying Doctors Service, Australia

Great Fundraising Organizations provides the key missing piece to achieving practical, sustainable, fundraising growth in the real world. By taking a deep dive into what makes an entire organization effective, it represents an important milestone in fundraising research. These proven strategies can transform your organization as they have done for so many others around the world."

—Russell N. James III, JD, PhD, CFP®
Professor & CH Foundation Chair in Personal Financial Planning
Director of Graduate Studies in Charitable Planning
Texas Tech University

"This book is magnificent. It's the book the charity sector needs right now! It needs to be seen by every staff member, board member . . . and donor! Anyone interested in working for or giving to a charity should read this – a wonderful insight into how charities do, and should, work. Early career fundraisers will get a blueprint for success. Senior, experienced fundraisers will feel seen and validated. And everyone will feel empowered, inspired, and energised for success!"

—Alex Hyde-Smith,
Chief Marketing Officer, Alzheimer's Society, UK

"What I love most about this great book is that it isn't only about theory, it's all about practice. Alan Clayton knows how to achieve great fundraising results because he's done it, over and over again. *Great Fundraising Organi-*

zations defines the essential ingredients, shows how to assemble them, then guides us through the process that makes the dream a reality. The result is Utopian fundraising success."

—**Ken Burnett,**
author, *Relationship Fundraising* and other books.

"Alan is my favourite fundraising expert and this book will make him one of yours as well! His hard-won vast knowledge and worldwide experience is passed onto you to help change the basic way you think about people, organizations, and creating world-beating fundraising ideas, processes, and results. Make no mistake he will change the way you see the world!"

—**Pat Dade,**
Founder Director, Cultural Dynamics Strategy and Marketing Ltd.

"We really truly believe we will beat macular disease now because of being a Great Fundraising organisation, and those with macular disease believe it too. Macular Society was an early adopter of the practice detailed in this book and we have seen tremendous growth as a result."

—**Emma Malcolm,**
Director of Fundraising & Marketing, Macular Society

GREAT FUNDRAISING ORGANIZATIONS

WHY AND HOW THE WORLD'S BEST CHARITIES EXCEL AT RAISING MONEY

ALAN CLAYTON

WILEY

Published by John Wiley & Sons, Inc., Hoboken, New Jersey.
Published simultaneously in Canada.

For general information on our other products and services or for technical support, please contact our Customer Care Department within the United States at (800) 762-2974, outside the United States at (317) 572-3993 or fax (317) 572-4002.

Wiley also publishes its books in a variety of electronic formats. Some content that appears in print may not be available in electronic formats. For more information about Wiley products, visit our web site at www.wiley.com.

Library of Congress Cataloging-in-Publication Data is Available:

ISBN: 9781394278251 (cloth)
ISBN: 9781394278268 (ePub)
ISBN: 9781394278275 (ePDF)

Cover Design and Image: Wiley
Author Photo: Revolutionise International, 2024

SKY10092492_120324

To Wee Kenny Burnett, who took a chance on a long shot

Contents

xi

Contents

Foreword

Many good things spring from fundraising conventions. There are usually a sprinkling of educational sessions that really resonate, and the plenary sessions can be genuinely inspiring and uplifting. But by far the most value conventions offer is the networking and the conversations they engender. And so it was with the Great Fundraising project. Born of a post-conference gin and tonic, what was initially a very simple idea morphed into a 10-year program of research, the most exciting scientific project I have ever been involved with and the generation of literally billions of dollars for nonprofits around the globe.

This is a book about how to achieve growth in fundraising, but not just growth per se – massive growth. Even back in 2012 we were beginning to understand a little of what made for good fundraising and best practices in a plethora of different channels and media. But no-one had very deliberately focused on organizations that had excelled in a more strategic sense: identifying an audacious goal, creating whole organizational buy-in for that goal, and then doubling, tripling, or even quadrupling income as a consequence. Just what was it about this handful of organizations that drove their success?

When Alan Clayton first commissioned the research, I thought we might end up with the seven habits of successful fundraising leaders or some such, a sense perhaps of how great fundraising leaders behaved and the pattern of actions that these leaders took to deliver success for their organization. There was certainly an element of this, but we ended up with much, much more.

There did appear to be some characteristics shared by our great fundraising leaders. They were certainly passionate about the causes they were working for, defining success not as their personal success but rather in terms of what the organization had achieved. They also had a steely belief that their audacious fundraising goals could be achieved and spent the majority of their time focused internally, getting the organization to the point where it was truly "fundraisable" and shared that belief too.

Our great fundraising leaders were uniquely focused on their teams, investing in their personal development, building their confidence, and in the case of more senior folks, grooming them to be great fundraising leaders in their own right. This approach to leadership engendered a high level of motivation, belief, and loyalty. Because of this, great fundraising teams did not suffer the churn that plagues most nonprofits. They were typically in place for five to seven years. They desired to see things through.

We also learned a lot about the culture of philanthropy built by our outstanding leaders. Notable here is the celebration of philanthropy. In my experience, most nonprofits are very good at celebrating mission success and what they achieve for the communities they serve. But they are less good at celebrating the philanthropy and the fundraisers that made those successes possible. Our great fundraising organizations were, and there was also a broader sense that their fundraisers would be acknowledged, valued, and rewarded for being the professionals they are. Key, too, to the notion of a philanthropic culture was a strong, unifying, and deeply emotional case for support. As I write that sentence it sounds so simple, yet of course it is not. Many organizations have a plethora of programs all of which are deemed important. So picking the right project, or more typically finding a way to synthesize the right projects to arrive at an appropriate case, can be laden with emotional baggage and fear of internal conflict. One of the central contributions of Alan's Great

Fundraising project is that it teaches a process for making the right choices and developing something so powerful it can be transformational for both team members and donors alike. All want to be a part of making it a reality.

We've certainly come a long way in the past decade, looking at great fundraising in multiple countries and through a variety of different lenses. We've also looked at the relationship between branding and fundraising, offering a new take on what adds value and how it might be enhanced. And our most recent project has looked at fundraisers, their well-being, their experiences of fundraising, and the things that most inspire (or demotivate) them in their roles. Great fundraising, as I have already explained, requires teams that see it through, so understanding what makes those teams tick is hugely important.

You're about to read a very personal take from Alan on the implications of all this research. Having data is one thing, but interpreting that data and turning it into something practical, quite another. In my experience, gathering data is the easy part. I will be forever grateful to Alan for allowing me to be a part of this project. It was certainly fulfilling to be given a window into so many great fundraising organizations, but I'm most grateful to have been witness to how the learning could then be leveraged to help others aspiring to that greatness – and to see the massive expansion of philanthropic income that resulted. In case study after case study, Alan continued to hone the best way to use these results and craft them into a unique yet simple process that could be adopted by all.

He also introduced me to the emotional space and the power of that in breaking down barriers between fundraising and other functions, creating buy-in right across an organization. You're about to experience a little of that emotion and to feel its power in a very intimate way as Alan tells the stories at the core of this project. It is important to reflect on how he makes you feel and why that feeling was so powerful for the focal organization and its stakeholders. As neuroscience now affirms, it is emotion that drives action, while logic leads only to conclusions. In all individuals' fundraising, emotion is important. In great fundraising, it is both fundamental and core.

Enjoy your journey in great fundraising.

Professor Adrian Sargeant
Institute for Sustainable Philanthropy
June 2024

"How Can It Be So Hard to Save a Child?"

This book is about growth.

The charities mentioned in these pages are part of a set that has raised billions. They have done so by implementing big-picture insights based on our research of the Great Fundraising Organizations to create transformational growth across the long term. These numbers are no exaggeration. The data exists and is in the public domain. More importantly, each organization has used its share of the billions to advance its mission and increase its services.

It is my earnest hope that by the end of this book, you will be on the path to raising billions too. Or millions, or thousands – whatever growth your organization's purpose demands of your fundraising.

But this story starts in another place entirely – it begins with a person I failed. Years ago, I knew a man who was an excellent aid worker in the Global South. He'd given up a very prestigious job in the United Kingdom to deliver aid at the front lines in some of the most devastated parts of the world. His work was phenomenal. But there came a point where he wanted a more settled life while still working and helping children, and so he decided fundraising might be the career for him.

At the time, I was the manager of a small but very effective fundraising team. We were looking to expand, and we got an application from this man. I was thrilled. This person was a pure-born fundraiser. He was a storyteller extraordinaire: he could meet people and tell them exactly what problem the nonprofit was addressing and what their donations could achieve. Plus, he was lovely to spend time with; he was one of the most present and caring but determined individuals you could come across. Soft-spoken but steely.

When he joined our organization, his work was great. Donors loved to spend time with him, and he generated significant gifts because his relationships with the donors were so powerful. But over time, I watched his morale drop.

As his line manager, I did what I could to support him. But each week, when we began our routine meeting, I could tell his faith and enthusiasm in fundraising was fading. He was finding it difficult to survive on the salary he was on. He couldn't get what he needed from the other departments in the organization to tell the donors the right stories to make them feel connected to the nonprofit. He was consistently being told off for his personal approach to fundraising and for how he communicated the organization's stories. He was being criticized by his peers despite his achievements. He was spending more time dealing with the internal politics of the organization than raising money.

Even now, after 25 years, it is gutting for me to tell this story. It was my responsibility as a fundraising leader to help him, and I was entirely unable to do so. I took him out to coffee one day to try to talk some faith into him, and he was depressed. I remember him sitting across from me, shoulders slumped, drinking his coffee slowly. He said, "Alan, all I want to do is a good thing. How can it be so hard to save a child?"

I was young and inexperienced in leadership at the time; I didn't have answers. Two weeks later, he left fundraising and moved back into aid work, where he's had a brilliant career. But here's the thing: he should have been the greatest fundraiser the world had ever seen. He had all the makings of one. Except I failed him. I didn't know how to give him what he needed to change the world.

It was the first time I had been directly in charge of someone with immense talent, and it was horrifying to me that he quit. He was lost and confused, struggling in a broken system, desperate to raise more money to do good and unable to do so, and I couldn't give him any answers.

But it became the catalyst I needed to go look for them.

Learning from the Best

For the next 25 years, I went on a quest to understand why it can be so hard to save a child and what we as fundraising leaders can do about it. Following my failure, I left the organization and decided to learn from the best. So I reached out to whom I considered to be the very best, Ken Burnett.

I was fortunate enough to be mentored by Ken for a decade, which probably makes me one of the luckiest fundraisers alive. He helped me grow from an angry young man to a somewhat immature but more stable middle-aged man. More importantly, he taught me that fundraising at its heart was about donors and not the organization. As he wrote in his 2002 book *Relationship Fundraising*, fundraising was where everyone could win, which meant it wasn't a necessary evil but a good thing in its own right. These were revolutionary insights that changed the way I approached my profession.

During that decade, I established my own agency. We had clients that were spectacularly successful, and we had some that struggled. Both successes and failures were important because I learned by comparing the two and finding patterns. I discovered that the differentiating factor between my clients that succeeded and those that struggled was the internal culture of the organization and their relationship with my agency. Clients that didn't do so well were often mired in internal conflict and kept us at a distance as a vendor. The ones that succeeded had a different approach. We were very much a part of their team, rather than just a supplier of communications and data.

This observation was confirmed by the very first bit of research I did. At the end of the decade, I was moving out of the agency and wasn't sure what to do next. So I sat down with each of our clients that we had worked with for a significant period of time and interviewed them about what they considered to be the critical success factors in their relationship with our agency. None of them said it was the creative communications or the analyses or the strategy work. Instead, they said it was mood, energy, focus, and chemistry: the symbiosis of our agency team and their people that created an effect on their internal culture, confidence, and the pace they could work at.

It was an incredible insight. I realized that people were not necessarily looking for another supplier of high-quality communications and data. They were looking for someone who could help them build the capacity, energy, and focus of their fundraising teams. I decided to not set up another agency and instead began to research acceleration. Since then, I have spent the last decade building Revolutionise International so we can accelerate people with purpose.

There are not a lot of books in the fundraising sector about acceleration, but there are plenty in the private sector. The more I learned, the more I could distinguish both parallels and differences between the private sector versus the nonprofit sector. We began to apply some of these insights to organizations with immediate effect and saw quite a few successes. More importantly, at this stage, we uncovered the primacy of emotion, both as a driver of growth and a blocker of it. I was still working with Ken Burnett at the time, and we ran a highly successful seminar series called "Emotional Fundraising."

I didn't know it then, but I was circling closer and closer to a unified approach and methodology. I couldn't see it as yet – the answers were fragmented, disjointed, the thesis unformed. That would change once I met Professor Adrian Sargeant.

Research on the Great Fundraising Organizations

Professor Sargeant was the foremost academic on fundraising in both the United Kingdom and the United States. He had been a professor of fundraising since 2001, and I've long regarded him as the go-to academic on the subject. We had never managed to have an in-depth chat until now, but I had extraordinary respect for his work.

I met Adrian for a single gin and tonic – one of the last drinks I would have, actually. We talked about his research for a bit, and then he asked what we were up to.

"Well," I said, "I think we've identified that the biggest driver of fundraising growth is behavioral."

Adrian put his glass down on the table and looked at me through the top half of his eyes. "Really?" he said.

"Well, we have no official research," I said, "so I cannot say we've identified it. But let's put it this way: it is more than a hunch."

"Any interest in getting that research?"

We had looked for existing data, of course, but there were no studies on the behaviors of the Great Fundraising Organizations. If we wanted scientific research and data, we would need to go out and conduct the studies ourselves.

Turns out Adrian was very keen to research the behaviors of the Great Fundraising Organizations compared to organizations that struggled or flatlined. The problem, he told me wryly, was getting funding for that kind of research.

So I went home and thought about it on my commute. By the end of that train ride, I had decided to fund the research. I had to pay the first installment of it personally because I didn't have a company vehicle at the time, but I knew it was important. This could change how we understood fundraising. It could be the catalyst that finally answered the question I had been asking these many years: *How can it be so hard to save a child, and what can we do about it?*

This first research study that we commissioned from Professor Sargeant, his partner Professor Jen Shang, and their team provided the insights that form the foundations for this book. Since then, over the years, we have commissioned several more rounds of academic research from Professor Sargeant and his team: into leadership, branding and communications, legacies, fundraiser recruitment, retention, and inspiration (i.e. fundraising team motivation). All our research reports can be downloaded on our organization website, Revolutionise International (revolutionise.com). We have also internally carried out a large set of action research: over 400 interviews with successful and unsuccessful organizations to understand what works. This action research is informal, but it was hugely insightful. Lastly, we have done detailed casework of more than a hundred organizations in over 20 countries.

Our first round of academic research focused on the Great Fundraising giants in the large Western economies, but since then, we have been diligent about looking at a wide range of organizations across a whole spectrum of causes, sizes, and geographies. We've worked with organizations from the Philippines to India to Argentina and from Serbia to Ethiopia to Namibia, with global UNICEF to regional Strømme Foundation fundraising in the southern tip of Norway, from the University of the Highlands and Islands, Scotland, to L'École Polytechnique de Lausanne, Switzerland, to St. Labre Indian School in Montana, United States, and from Feed the Children, United States, to Ikamva Labantu, South Africa. We've partnered with museums, research institutions, INGOs, social entrepreneurs, gastroenterologists, and civil rights movements – and a lot more in between these extremes. From this varied research, we have collected hard data that forms the source material for everything you will read in this book.

So what did that first study reveal?

Discovering the Red Dot

According to our parameters, a Great Fundraising Organization fulfills three criteria:

- Transformational growth: To qualify as a Great Fundraising Organization, it is not sufficient to inherit a big fundraising program and be good at managing it. The growth we were looking at was growth with purpose; this means the organizations were expanding at a significant enough level to impact the purpose or mission of the organization. In other words, growth that simply covered existing liabilities did not count; it had to be growth that went toward making the world a better place.

- Sustainable growth: We were looking for growth that lasted, not a one-hit, one-year wonder. There are often brilliant fundraising initiatives, the most famous of which is the ice bucket challenge that raised $250 million or more. We are not dismissing the incredible impact of these initiatives on an organization, but we wanted to measure long-term and sustainable growth rather than one-off.

- Purpose-driven growth: Great Fundraising Organizations engineer and experience growth that is driven by the purpose of their organization, i.e. the problem they were established as a nonprofit to solve. This means that the people donating to a Great Fundraising Organization have fully bought into the nonprofit's mission. There is another form of fundraising, which is to annoy people until they give you money, but we were looking at those organizations that managed to attract true believers.

So Great Fundraising Organizations, according to our parameters, experienced transformational, sustainable, and purpose-driven growth. The first question we asked ourselves was, *How did that growth happen?*

When we looked at the numbers and data, we realized that Great Fundraising Organizations experienced what we called surges of growth. It was never a straight line or smooth graph of upward expansion when viewed across a long-enough timescale. There would be periods of rapid growth, then a period of flatlining or modest decline before another surge of growth.

It is interesting to note that these periods of flatlining or decline did not coincide with economic factors. They weren't caused by economic instability or recession. Likewise, surges were not created by economic booms. There was no correlation with the state of the economy. This pattern seemed to be solely organization driven.

Similarly, the timescale of the growth or flatlining was unique to each Great Fundraising Organization. The bigger organizations could have a growth surge that was 10 years long before flatlining, mid-size organizations usually maintained a growth surge across 4 to 5 years, and the smaller organizations flatlined and then surged again within 2 years. But the shape was always the same: surge, then dip or flatline, and then surge again.

So we asked ourselves: *What was the difference in the organization when it was growing versus when it was flatlining?* We were lucky enough to study the growth of some of the Great Fundraising Organizations for a substantial period, about 20–30 years, which allowed us to examine continuity, and we interviewed people at these organizations to understand what was changing between the growth and decline phases. It rapidly became obvious that the difference between when the organization was growing versus struggling was the internal state of the nonprofit. During a surge, they were focused and energized. When the nonprofit was flatlining, they were tired and confused.

Every time a Great Fundraising Organization came to the end of a surge and began to struggle, the great fundraising leaders, intuitively, began creating focus and energy again to create another surge.

When you look back over the research, it becomes very clear that all these leaders were using an extremely consistent but not realized methodology. They hadn't articulated this methodology to themselves; they were simply executing it based on instinct, shaped by their experience and abilities.

The data shows there are two key elements to creating this shift in mood:

1. When an organization was flatlining (i.e. tired or confused), they tended to look inward, at their structures and processes. When an organization was growing (i.e. focused and vitalized), they got their energy from having a single, external goal or dream that helped them focus on solving the bigger problem they wanted to eradicate in the world (i.e. their purpose).

2. When the mood shifted from confused and tired to focused and energized, it switched in a single moment. We called this moment the "Red Dot."

The Red Dot is crucial for Great Fundraising Organizations. The dots you see in Figure I.1 are all Red Dot moments, each signaling a switch from decline to a surge of growth.

The Red Dot is a moment in time. It is a board meeting where the board makes three key decisions that are required to create a massive surge of growth. But what *leads up* to that board meeting is an in-depth set of internal changes in the organization that give the board the confidence to make these three decisions, and that gives the organization its focus and energy back.

This is what this book is about. Throughout the following chapters, we will show you how to change your organization to create focus and energy so you can trigger that Red Dot moment and create a surge of growth – and then, exactly like the Great Fundraising Organizations, once that surge has ended, do it all over again.

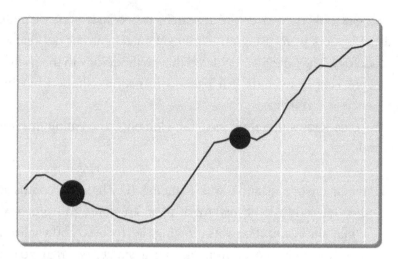

Figure I.1   The Red Dot.
Source: Revolutionise International Limited 2024.

Turning Intuition into Methodology

The methodology you will encounter in this book has been created by turning the instincts and insights of the great fundraising leaders, along with research, data, and testing, into a process that any nonprofit can follow. Creating this methodology was an iterative process over the years.

In early 2013, I knew the question we were asking was: *How do you trigger transformational growth in an organization?* So I took the research that Professors Sargeant and Shang did for us into the desert in Arizona for a month, and I sat and studied it so that I could put it into a format that would be useful for fundraising leaders based on experience and casework.

Since then, for 12 years, our team at Revolutionise International has put that format into action. We have worked with many organizations, some of which stalled but many of which succeeded. Based on this action research, we commissioned further studies from

Professors Sargeant and Shang (those several rounds of academic research we mentioned, plus the casework), and we have introduced a structured learning process into our own organization so we can add more detail to our learnings, month by month and quarter by quarter, which allows us to be granular about specific actions and behaviors. All our results have been guided by our academic research. You will read many of the client success stories in this book.

We learned that what distinguishes a Great Fundraising Organization from others is how the nonprofit behaves with regard to fundraising. Externally, the only limit on a fundraising team is their total market universe. Cancer, for example, has a very big market in most countries, while other causes, like macular disease, may have smaller markets. But excluding the total market universe, the key driver for growth was internal behavior.

It didn't matter if the organization was big or small or what country they operated in. Despite cultural, linguistic, and local employment differences, there were certain key behaviors that triggered a Red Dot. These behaviors were universal; they applied to organizations as big as UNICEF and as small as a local community foundation in South Island, New Zealand. In every case, they led to growth.

Figure I.2 shows a sample of organizations we have worked with to implement our findings on the Great Fundraising Organizations. They are selected to show that the behaviors that lead to growth are independent of size, geography, or cause. In fact, the independence of country is such a significant insight that we have invested in Fundraising World (fundraisingworld.com), run by Howard Lake and Connor Seaton, to facilitate worldwide knowledge and skill-share and learning.

There are a few assumptions and decisions that can help you understand our data. Since this is a book about growth, most of our numbers are quoted in percentage growth of top-line revenue. There is no doubt that the profit created by fundraising – i.e. the absolute

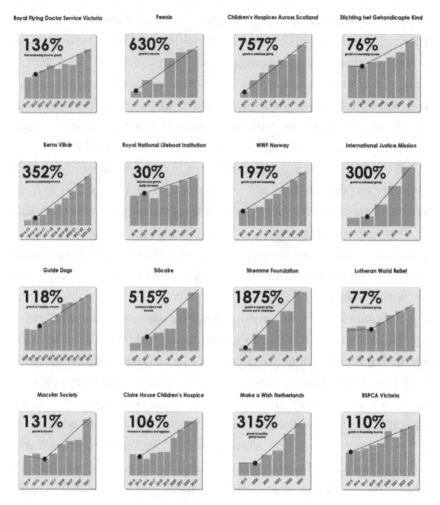

Figure I.2 Growth charts for a selection of Great Fundraising Organizations.

Source: Revolutionise International Limited 2024.

value of the money spent on the organization's purpose – is the most important aspect of fundraising, but this is not what we are measuring. We are measuring growth, not profit, which is why our numbers are percentage growth of top-line revenue.

Secondly, most of the case studies in this book are at least five years old because otherwise we would not have been able to measure sustainable growth accurately. We have many more organizations working with us that are earlier in their journeys, but we cannot include their data because we need a good five years. Some of these organizations are rolling out at scale, such as Make a Wish International, which has provided their bespoke version of Great Fundraising education to their multiple country affiliates. Make a Wish Netherlands was the pioneer of this program before the international office picked it up and has achieved 315% growth in their monthly giving program in three years. Others are following their lead, with Canada poised to be the next mover.

What You Can Expect from This Book

If you are a fundraising director looking to plug a short-term deficit in your nonprofit or make more money by next month, then this is not the book for you. If, however, you are looking for a methodology on how to transform your nonprofit to break that fundraising ceiling and create long-term, sustainable, and transformational growth, then you are in the right place.

Transformational growth requires you to first transform your organization by bringing in energy and focus through behavioral change. The following chapters will *not* offer you advice on how to execute the details of fundraising, but they will show you how to systematically and culturally build a Great Fundraising Organization to trigger a Red Dot. Our focus is on the big picture, not on the minute.

This is also a book about leadership. Focus and energy in an organization come from behavior and belief, and the root of behavior and belief is good fundraising leadership. Ultimately, this is a book about how you can develop your leadership skills and abilities to create focus and energy to build a Great Fundraising Organization. It is about how you can create an environment and give your team the tools they need to change the world. I was given my first fundraising leadership job 25 years ago, and I failed at it. I never want you to feel the same.

Moreover, this is a book about emotions. One of the questions we had to ask ourselves when analyzing the research was, *Is there a difference between leading a fundraising organization and any other commercial venture?* The answer was a resounding yes, and the differentiator was the significance of emotions in fundraising. People donate for emotional reasons. The reason your organization was founded is emotional (someone wanted to make the world a better place). The reasons why people get focused and vitalized or tired and discouraged are all emotional. At the end of the day, a fundraising business is supported by data, logic, analysis, and structures, but it is driven by an emotional need and an emotional solution. So on top of the analytical work one needs to be trained in and excel at, you must also strive for emotional excellence. Emotions drive behavior, which drives growth.

This book is divided into two parts. Part I will deal with the research-based underpinnings of the Red Dot. We'll explore a key insight that all Great Fundraising Organizations know about themselves and how they harness that insight to accelerate growth. We'll then break down the components of the Red Dot – the set of internal changes that lead up to the Red Dot moment that we call the Trifecta – so you can see how these Great Fundraising Organizations consistently accelerate growth. We'll do this with all the evidence and case studies so you can see these teachings in action.

If Part I is the structural foundation of the book, then Part II delves into emotional excellence. We've found that our clients need the practical information first so they can learn to trust what we are telling them. But once they do, they progress into the emotional space, which is where all the conflict and the roadblocks reside. At the end of the day, emotions are why we do things. Logic is why we don't.

During the course of this book, you will encounter some very uncomfortable truths. Much of what you read may challenge the accepted wisdom you have learned over your years as a professional fundraiser; it may feel disconcerting to encounter. I wouldn't blame you if it did. But this work has been mapped, replicated, and tested. In a world where thousands of books and articles tell you how fundraising should work or could work in a perfect world, this book tells you how it *does* work in the real world. These truths may be uncomfortable, but they are necessary. If you can move past your discomfort into a space of openness, then you can find what you came to this book seeking: answers.

The Delight of Doing a Good Thing

There is delight in doing a good thing.

If you are successful in driving fundraising growth over an extended period of time by following the insights in this book, say at least 10 years, then you will have made the world a better place. How? Over that period, you will have grown your organization's income, which means the spend of your organization increases, which means the lives of your service users will be better in large numbers, leaving the world in a better place than you found it. This happens so gradually that you may not notice, but a decade after you transform your organization into a Great Fundraising Organization, you will be able to look back and say, *I played a small part in changing the world.* I have watched this happen in my career to the people I know and work with, and it is one of the most incredible feelings. More importantly, it is what gives your career meaning in the long term.

Before this, however – say in about five years – you will notice that your actions have created sustainable, long-term results. There is an enhanced and sustainable impact on your organization that will be exhilarating to witness.

Prior to this, say in about two to three years, you will experience the high of short-term results. This book is about long-term growth, yes, but we have seen that the moment you introduce focus and energy into an organization, there is always a measurable impact on short-term fundraising. It gives you and your team a wonderful buzz.

Before that buzz, you will experience the satisfaction of a Red Dot moment. It can be hard to get there, but you will reach that moment in time when you will be able to relaunch your fundraising program with renewed vitality. It is a huge achievement in its own right, and it feels like one.

Move back in time again, to you *working* toward the Red Dot. During this period, if you can execute everything we have shown you in this book, you will be able to bring your whole organization into a state of renewed belief, confidence, and alignment. There will be a feeling of shared purpose and of belonging.

Now move back in time once more, to the moment when you finish this book. By the Conclusion, you will have a clear understanding of a set of decisions that drive the behaviors your organization needs. If you are like the fundraiser I was responsible for, slumped over his coffee with many questions and no answers; if you are like me 25 years ago before I began my quest, wanting to make the world a better place but not knowing how and confused about how to lead my team; if you are a tired fundraising director who has hit their financial ceiling and does not know how to break it; or even if you are already successful and simply want to raise the bar in pursuit of your mission, then this book will offer you simplicity from the complexity you are facing. You will close the book with a clear knowledge of how to move forward. You will have clarity.

This is not a book about fundraising. It is a book about how to lead so that you can accelerate growth and make the world a better place, faster. You begin by turning the page.

Part I

Triggering the Red Dot

Chapter 1

Two Businesses, One Mission

In the 2010s, an international nonprofit called CBM (formerly Christian Blind Mission), which works in the field of disabilities and in particular to eliminate preventable blindness in developing countries, decided to convert their irregular donors into regular monthly donors. These were people who gave to the charity in small amounts, at odd intervals, and to a number of charities, which placed them in a marketing segment unofficially referred to as "low value, infrequent, and promiscuous" (yes, that's a horrible nickname for a segment). Telephone fundraisers were asked to call these donors and encourage them to switch to automated donations via monthly direct debit.

One such telephone fundraiser – let's call him Paul – was dialing the number of an elderly donor named Marjorie. Marjorie lived in the Australian Outback and had been giving money to CBM for many years, but she gave it in old-fashioned ways. Sometimes she would send a check. Occasionally she would arrive at the Melbourne office with cash. Other times she would phone in and donate. There was no pattern to her donations; it could be spontaneous or a response to a direct appeal. It was also different amounts of money each time. Here's the thing about Marjorie, though: no matter how or when, she always donated. It was clear she cared, which made her a valuable supporter.

When Marjorie picked up the phone, Paul had his script ready. He explained to her that regular donations of a fixed amount helped nonprofits plan their finances better. If Marjorie switched to automated payments, it would also be easier for her. She wouldn't have to travel to the office or wait to get someone on the phone; she didn't need to write a check or withdraw cash. It would just go from her account every month, and she would never have to think about it. Wasn't that lovely?

There was a pause.

"Oh," Marjorie said, and she sounded sad. "That's a shame. I quite like calling and going to the office. I have nobody else to speak to."

Paul could sense there was more to this story, so he went off-script to discover more about Marjorie. It turns out, Marjorie was almost 90 years old. Her husband had passed away, her son had moved out, and her income was her pension. There were really only two things Marjorie did: she bought groceries and she donated to charity. Those were her basic needs. The reason she didn't give the same amount to charity each time was because the cost of groceries kept rising, and so she never knew how much money she would have left at the end of the month to donate. And the reason she donated in old-fashioned ways? Because Marjorie was lonely, and she craved the human contact that interacting with CBM and other nonprofits gave her.

When Paul hung up, he didn't transfer Marjorie to direct debit. Instead, he made a note on her file: *Be nice to Marjorie when she calls. She's a wonderful person.*

I first heard this story in 2014. Both Marjorie's and Paul's names have been changed, of course, but the person telling it to me was Paul himself, a man in his early twenties. We were in CBM's Melbourne office, in one of those cookie-cutter boardrooms: a big table in the center, a nondescript carpet. I was giving a seminar with their senior leadership and select members of the team. I had asked them to tell me about their donors, to which they responded, "They're elderly Australian women." That's a poor answer, of course; it tells you nothing. So Paul stood up and told this story.

When he was done, the room fell silent. You could almost hear the *thunk* of the penny dropping. *Low value, infrequent, promiscuous.* That may have been the nickname of the marketing segment Marjorie belonged to, but those words didn't apply to Marjorie. She was a good human being trying to do the best she could.

Heath McSolvin, the head of fundraising at CBM at the time, was incredibly moved by the story. "From now on," he said softly, "we have two missions. The first mission hasn't changed: it is to make sure we eliminate preventable blindness around the world. The second mission is that when Marjorie dies, she must do so knowing she was a wonderful person who made a difference and that her sacrifices counted for something. Marjorie must die knowing her life was worth living."

Most fundraising organizations believe they are one business with one mission. This mission is usually the reason they were established (for example, to help disabled people, or save drowning sailors, or give end-of-life care to dying children). Fundraising, they believe, is a simple matter of telling people how good they are at this purpose – how many disabled people they've helped or sailors they've saved – and the money will come pouring in.

In other words, most nonprofit organizations focus exclusively on their service users to the exclusion of all else.

But what McSolvin stumbled upon that day, albeit unknowingly, is that fundraising organizations have a *second* business: one that is focused on their donors. It's the business of meeting a donor's basic need to give. It's the business that tells the Marjories of the world that they matter. The Great Fundraising Organizations recognize they are *two* businesses in one, united by a common mission. One business is meeting the needs of their service users, and the other is meeting the needs of their donors.

This insight is fundamental to becoming a Great Fundraising Organization. I would even go as far as to say it is the foundation of everything in this book, the learning that unlocks how or why nonprofits succeed or fail. Because once you understand that you are two businesses instead of one, you realize those businesses *conflict* with each other more often than not. Managing that conflict and aligning is how you accelerate growth.

Two Businesses

The story of how we identified that a fundraising nonprofit is two businesses in one is circuitous. When I first got the research on Great Fundraising Organizations from Professors Sargeant and Shang, the one thing that leaped out at me was that great fundraising leaders were spending no more than 50% of their time actively raising money.

Only 50%? That seemed counterintuitive. What were they doing with the rest of their time?

As I was mulling over this, I met someone at my golf club who was very senior in sales at Hewlett-Packard. We played golf and chatted about work, and I told him about the interesting puzzle we'd found in the data: the great fundraising leaders, the people who consistently attracted incredible revenue for their organizations, were only spending half of their time fundraising. It didn't make any sense.

The senior sales executive wasn't puzzled at all. "It makes complete sense," he said. "That's just like me!"

He explained that a junior salesperson spent 100% of their time selling. But when you got to his level, which was very high up at Hewlett-Packard, you spent half of your time selling and the other half explaining to the company what the client wanted. If he didn't, product design would give him printers that nobody would buy because the printers didn't meet their needs. So he spent 50% of this time making sales and the other 50% trying to get his company to make better products for their customers.

It was a lightbulb moment. What if we were looking at this wrong? What if, like the senior sales executive, the great fundraising leaders understood that they had *two* different functions and they had to divide their time between the two? The first function was fundraising from donors, similar to my golf friend selling Hewlett-Packard products to their customers. The second function was explaining what the donor wanted to the rest of the organization *so that* the great fundraising leaders could raise money (similar to my golf friend getting the right printers made to match his clients' requirements).

If this was true, what did it say about the organizational structure of a nonprofit?

We went back to the dataset with a new perspective and tested our observations. What we discovered is that unsuccessful fundraising organizations believed that they only served one set of customers, which was their service users. According to their organizational worldview, every pound, dollar, yen, and rupee should be spent meeting the needs of these service users. Any penny spent elsewhere was a waste of money.

Furthermore, in the worst organizations, the people who gave them this money (i.e. the donors) were relegated to subhuman status. They were seen as a hindrance, an irritating roadblock to accelerating growth. *Why won't they give us more? Why don't they just shut up and donate? Why do we need to spend money to get them to give? Why do we need to waste time and money saying thank you?* There was a

One set of customers

Figure 1.1   One set of customers.
Source: Revolutionise International Limited 2024.

huge naivety about how fundraising worked; it was believed that if the organization was good at fulfilling their purpose, people would be falling over themselves to donate.

What was even more surprising is that this perspective existed at every level of the organization, right from the juniors to senior leadership and the board. Experience made no difference. As far as they were concerned, fundraising should work like magic: snap your fingers and the money is here.

But of course, fundraising cannot thrive under these circumstances. It became a vicious cycle: the less money the fundraising department brought in, the more resentment built across the organization. *Why aren't donors giving? Why can't fundraising create more revenue? Why are we being held back from doing good in the world by something as silly as money?* I would go as far as to say that this worldview created toxicity when it came to the subject of money and the people who give it.

Our research showed that the Great Fundraising Organizations, on the other hand, believed they had two sets of customers: the donors and the service users. To succeed, they needed to be the best in the market at meeting the needs of both. Clearly, you can't be a Great Fundraising Organization if you don't meet the needs of your service users. But equally, you need to meet the needs of your donors – *and*

Two sets of customers

The Great Fundraising Organization excels
at meeting the needs of both.

Figure 1.2 Two sets of customers.
Source: Revolutionise International Limited 2024.

be better at it than other organizations. If you aren't, someone else will meet their needs, and the money will go to them instead.

The best fundraising organizations, the ones that were inspiring, saw no friction between their two functions. Yes, meeting the needs of their service users made the world a better place, and that was a beautiful thing. But it was equally beautiful to make donors like Marjorie feel fulfilled, to let them know they were good people who did good things. A Great Fundraising Organization is the best at both.

But to meet the needs of both sets of customers, you have to recognize that these needs are vastly different. This is true even if the service user and the donor are the same person (which can happen, on occasion). The need to receive is very different from the need to give. If you don't treat them as distinct, you'll fail at both.

This means that an organization is consistently providing services to two different customer groups, and those services have to be distinct to match the group's needs. You cannot package the same product in the same way for two customer bases that don't align.

Trócaire is a long-term development nonprofit in Ireland that focuses on anti-oppression; they work in countries across Africa,

Two sets of customers

Figure 1.3 Two sets of customers, explained.
Source: Revolutionise International Limited 2024.

Asia, and Central America. When they came to us, their revenue had been slowly dropping and they couldn't understand why. Their slogan at the time – i.e. the message they were sending out to donors – was "Trócaire: Join the Fight for Justice."

On the surface, this looks great, doesn't it? They're an anti-oppression organization, so they're inviting their donors to join their journey to bring justice to every corner of the world. Perfect.

Except their donors are predominantly older Catholic women in Ireland. They don't want to fight anybody. "Justice" is not a word in their lexicon; they're elderly Christians, not human rights professionals.

This is a classic example of unwittingly selling the wrong product to the wrong people. "Join the Fight for Justice" is messaging that works perfectly for the passionate group of highly ethical professionals within Trócaire. It's why *they* joined the organization, and it's what *they* are trying to achieve for their service users. It doesn't meet the needs of their donors. In fact, Trócaire's main call to action was even more misguided. It said, "When you donate to Trócaire, you don't just give." Now they were actively telling their donors that money wasn't enough. To be valuable, the donors must join the fight for justice.

We worked with Trócaire to find better messaging that served the needs of their donors. What we ended up with was "Trócaire: Until Love Conquers Fear." We realized that the common problem across all Trócaire projects was fear. Their service users were being marginalized, controlled, and impoverished through the use of fear. If you're Christian, there is only one thing that can overcome fear. Some people call it "God," others "charity," still others call it "love," but they are translations of the same sentiment. We ran these words past Trócaire as options before settling on "love." The new messaging changed Trócaire's language of international development to theological language – and spoke directly to the audience they were trying to reach.

Trócaire's talented and driven new director of marketing and fundraising, Gwen Dempsey, jumped on the new focus and messaging and rapidly achieved culture change and the optimum investment. Revenue immediately returned to growth and, over the next six years, ably supported by the newly recruited Colin Skehan, achieved transformational growth. In the critical individual donor program, the growth achieved was 515% over five years.

This is what it means to sell the right product to the right people. To become a Great Fundraising Organization, you have to get to know your donors as people, to respect and care for them as individuals in their own right with their own thoughts and needs, rather than only as data points, marketing segments, or sources of

Trōcaire

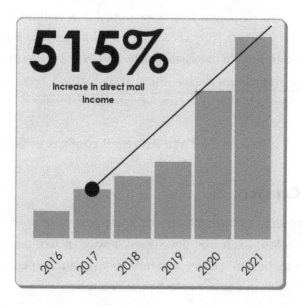

Figure 1.4 Trócaire growth chart.
Source: Revolutionise International Limited 2024.

money. Great Fundraising Organizations learn how to communicate with donors in the language that donors relate to.

Three Conflicts

Once you realize that every nonprofit is two businesses with one mission, you begin to see how the tensions in an organization stem from this intrinsic divide. It creates structural conflicts, of which we can identify three that are common for every organization in the world:

- Cultural conflict
- Investment conflict
- Communications conflict

I want to be clear that these structural conflicts are inevitable. A nonprofit is two disparate businesses, and it is natural for them to clash with each other. They *should* be at odds because they are fundamentally different. What distinguishes a Great Fundraising Organization from the others is that they have learned how to navigate these clashes such that they are constructive tensions, rather than destructive conflicts.

Let's take a look at the three structural conflicts in detail.

Cultural Conflict

The fundraising department doesn't share a culture with the rest of the organization. Each has developed a way of working that helps them execute their functions, and in turn, they attract people that can effectively hold up and represent those cultures.

The nonfundraising departments exist in a culture that is a blend of the academic, scientific, and public sectors. We call this the ethical intellectual culture, and their purpose is to deliver quality services and minimize risk. In other words, they keep people safe.

Being risk-averse when one is trying to save the world is a good thing; it is entirely appropriate and the best way for ethical intellectuals to achieve their goals. No one wants a doctor who loves risk. If ethical intellectuals make mistakes, people suffer or even die, so they're careful to be thorough and detail oriented. They rely on processes to avoid error, work closely with the evidence, and make decisions by consensus to ensure everything is thought-through and they've taken multiple points of view into account.

They are also incredibly driven to make the world a better place. Their view on money tends to be distant; their usual sources of money are grants, either from governments or foundations and research bodies, which means they see money as arriving from a fairly amorphous external source that isn't human.

These are amazing people: very driven, very loyal, and highly ethical. If they have one drawback, it is that their worldview tends to make them judgmental of other cultures. They believe that if they could just educate everyone to become an ethical intellectual like themselves, the world would be better.

They are also wary of emotion. People in this culture have been professionally trained to emotionally detach from work for two reasons. First, it is so that they can survive on a day-to-day basis despite the trauma and pain they are exposed to in this line of work. And second, it is because emotions can cloud judgment as well as drive hasty decisions, and they need rational, evidence-based, and precise decision-making to do their job well.

Successful fundraising departments, on the other hand, have a dichotomous culture to the ethical intellectuals. They are more similar to what we call ambitious achievers. These people are generally competitive. They need challenge and ambition; they enjoy standing out when it comes to meeting targets and in comparison to peers.

31

Two businesses, two cultures

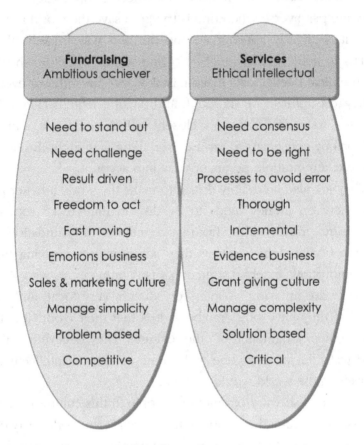

Fundraising Ambitious achiever	**Services** Ethical intellectual
Need to stand out	Need consensus
Need challenge	Need to be right
Result driven	Processes to avoid error
Freedom to act	Thorough
Fast moving	Incremental
Emotions business	Evidence business
Sales & marketing culture	Grant giving culture
Manage simplicity	Manage complexity
Problem based	Solution based
Competitive	Critical

Figure 1.5 The nonprofit culture clash.
Source: Revolutionise International Limited 2024.

They are also in the business of managing simplicity. Their job is to take the work of the services department and extract the simplicity and emotion from it.

You can see how this would create an immediate cultural conflict. On one hand, you have a fast-moving, competitive, emotions-based business (the fundraisers), and on the other hand, you have an incrementally improved, evidence-based business that, to make matters worse, doesn't have a lot of respect for emotions (the services departments, aka the ethical intellectuals). It leads to tension, and if not managed, that tension can grind a nonprofit to a halt.

Investment Conflict

The investment conflict is a conflict of timescales.

Services departments – i.e. the ethical intellectuals – typically manage their money like grant-receiving bodies. This means they work in yearly budgets or across three-year plans because this is how governments and foundations give out their money. Their full focus, when it comes to investment, is on the short-term.

The fundraising department, however, functions on long-term budgets because this is the best way to measure the lifetime value of the donor base. By long-term, we mean 5- to 7- to 10-year plans and projections.

The problem? Fundraising departments don't do well if only measured over the short-term. It's simply not where they thrive. But if they are allowed to think and act in the long-term, they can achieve exponential growth.

A consultant in the United Kingdom, Giles Pegram, ran a research study on precisely this. He studied more than 30 representative organizations to find out the relative investment effectiveness of the simplest form of fundraising, versus the performance of the equivalent amount of money in the stock market across a 14-year period.

He found that if you invested $1 million in the stock market, starting from the year 2000, the return on that $1 million would be around $400,000 after 14 years. This means that the compound effect of charity reserves left in investments was a return of 40%.

He then looked at what would happen if that same amount of money, instead of being kept in reserve, was invested in fundraising to get people to sign up for direct debit giving (which is the simplest form of fundraising). He found that for the first one or two years, the investment value dropped. But from the second year onwards, it started growing – and kept growing.

By the end of 14 years, the direct return on the same $1 million invested was 12 times more for fundraising than it was for the stock market. Twelve times. Let that sink in.

We've since reviewed these numbers across multiple organizations, and we've found that the shape of this graph stays exactly the same even if the absolute amounts vary with market conditions and time. And this is only the direct return. The indirect return of fundraising is much bigger than this because many of the people convinced to sign on for direct debit giving will upgrade the amount they are

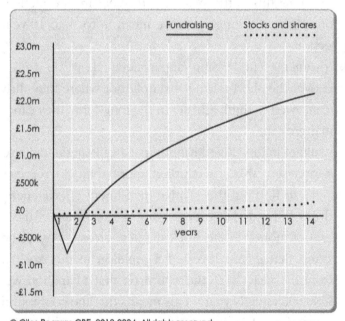

Figure 1.6 Giles Pegram's study.

Source: Reprinted with permission from Giles Pegram CBE, 2012–2024. All rights reserved.

willing to give over the years. Some of them will have passed away and left a legacy to the organization. So the real return is likely 25–30 times as much as the return in the stock market.

The evidence is clear: fundraising does not thrive in a knee-jerk perspective of the short-term. But if fundraising is allowed to function on a long-term horizon, there is no doubt in my mind that investing in fundraising is the best return an organization will ever get.

Unfortunately, most nonprofits tie their fundraising departments to one-year or three-year budgets. This means that in organizations that fail, fundraising is unable to look at the first year (which is the year in which they invest money) independent of the budgetary requirements of the other departments. Of course, if one looks only at that first year in Pegram's study, investing in fundraising becomes a difficult decision. It is a much more straightforward decision if you look at the long-term results.

Communications Conflict

By "communications," we don't mean internal communications within an organization but the messaging created to convey to donors what a nonprofit does and why donors should be giving them their hard-earned money. The communications conflict is a big one; our recent research suggests that it is one of the reasons why fundraisers resign from their positions, which is a major issue in the global nonprofit sector.

So what is the communications conflict? In simple terms, it is a difference in how the two businesses need to convey the essential purpose of their nonprofit to meet the needs of their customers.

The services departments trade on credibility. It is what they rely on to encourage service users to trust them and come forward to receive their services. It is also how they recruit new staff. Similarly, they trade on credibility when communicating with foundations, governments, or grant-giving bodies, as this is the criterion on which they are evaluated. It stands to reason, then, that the communications they create would focus on the organization's work, as well as the outcomes they achieved, and would use hard data in the form of statistics and evidence to back this up. In other words, communications created by ethical intellectuals are designed to project credibility and focus on the organization's solution to the problem.

The fundraising department, however, trades in empathy. "Empathy" is sometimes used to mean "sympathy" or "pity," but this isn't the correct definition of the term. It means the sharing of emotions. Our

Two businesses, different communications

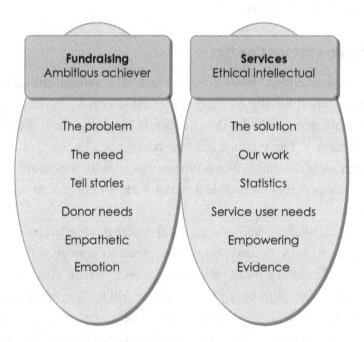

Fundraising Ambitious achiever	Services Ethical intellectual
The problem	The solution
The need	Our work
Tell stories	Statistics
Donor needs	Service user needs
Empathetic	Empowering
Emotion	Evidence

Figure 1.7   Two businesses, different communications.
Source: Revolutionise International Limited 2024.

data sources around the world say that fundraising needs to create empathy to work. It needs to tell stories, and it must operate in an emotional space to meet the needs of donors. It must focus on the problem.

When the communications conflict is not managed or understood, the fundraising department can end up with messaging that doesn't help them raise funds. This is exactly the problem we saw with Trócaire earlier in the chapter. The communications created by the marketing team or the rest of the organization speak to the credibility of the nonprofit and what the services department wants the donor to want, but it doesn't speak to the donors themselves. The fundraising department cannot do their job with that messaging, which leads to frustration. Meanwhile, the rest of the organization wonders why fundraising cannot meet targets and attract more revenue.

Be the Best at Both

So, you have two businesses with one mission, and it creates conflicts that run right down the center of your organization. How do you get these businesses to work side by side to resolve the three main conflicts? How do you turn what can be potentially destructive into creative tensions that push your nonprofit to greater heights?

The first thing you should *not* do is try to eliminate the conflict. Our research shows that unsuccessful organizations try to break down the silos and get everyone to work together as a team; that means one culture, one investment strategy, and one type of communications. This is counterproductive. The two businesses are silos because they fulfill two very different functions for two distinct customer bases. Eradicating the silos and trying to find a halfway point between them simply dilutes those functions, and doesn't allow either business to fulfill their goals properly.

Remember, the Great Fundraising Organizations recognize that they have to be the best at *both* businesses to succeed – and that means allowing each business to thrive as itself. The two parts of a nonprofit need to interact and engage with each other, but they do not need to share the same culture with the same behaviors. Compromise is the death of your fundraising.

What you *should* do is get your silos working cooperatively and constructively without cross-infecting each other. You do this by focusing on internal alignment, which means you search for emotional solutions to emotional problems and cultural solutions to cultural problems. Internal alignment can be created in three ways: respect and dialogue, education, and a shared ambition.

Respect and Dialogue

The cultural conflict can grind a nonprofit to a halt when the mutual incompatibility between the fundraising department (i.e. the ambitious achievers) and the services departments (i.e. the ethical intellectuals) gets out of hand. The fundraising department finds the services departments slow to respond and their work dry; they are consistently frustrated by the lack of emotion in the data and products they are given, as well as by how long it takes to get anything done. Meanwhile, the services departments are wary of emotion and have a general dislike of fundraising. They chafe against the fact that the ambitious achievers are always in a rush and are simplifying the ethical intellectuals' complex work. If left unattended, this incompatibility can deepen into distaste and derision.

Respect is key to solving this. Our research shows that the Great Fundraising Organizations foster professional respect between the two cultures, particularly with an eye to celebrating their differences. In a Great Fundraising Organization, both businesses acknowledge that the other has a different but equally important skill set without which the organization cannot succeed.

Respect goes hand in hand with dialogue. The one simple solution that the Great Fundraising Organizations implement – and I cannot believe we had to spend money to discover this – is that they ensure both businesses talk to each other. They establish real dialogue. In organizations that struggled or flatlined, issues were addressed by memoranda or "reply all" emails (which are particularly toxic). In successful organizations, both cultures sat down in groups and worked through their issues so that each business was empowered to fulfill their functions.

Education

In many ways, the investment conflict is similar to the trolley problem. In the trolley problem, you have seven people working on one trolley track and one person working on another while a trolley hurtles toward them with no means of stopping. You, as station master, have the power to switch tracks – so you can choose to save one person or save seven.

In nonprofit organizations, investing in fundraising can often feel like choosing between saving one life or saving many. In organizations that stall, fundraising departments have to convince the rest of the charity that their growth and results cannot be measured by a single year – they need to be seen across a much longer time horizon. To achieve that longer time horizon, the organization needs to keep investing in fundraising.

But for the CEOs and the boards of those organizations, this choice is difficult to make. Why should they pour money into a strategy that is showing no immediate results when they can use that money to save a life? This is the most common answer fundraising departments get when they ask for investment: *We can't spend the money on fundraising right now because we need to save lives.*

I understand the conundrum, and I think it is one of the most difficult decisions a leader must make. But as Pegram's study showed us, investing in fundraising gives us the opportunity to save many more lives by order of magnitude.

The problem in organizations that struggle is that the only people who understand how fundraising investment works are in the fundraising department. No one else in the organization realizes that fundraising works across larger timescales; thus, no one else understands that fundraising investment can save more lives in the future.

The solution to this is education. If the people being asked to authorize fundraising investment are educated in how that investment works, and if they are kept informed of progress, then they are much more likely to buy into the bigger picture and be cooperative with the fundraising department's needs. This, of course, includes the senior leadership team from all departments, the CEO, and the board. Organization-wide understanding and involvement in creating investments and, critically, monitoring and testing these investments as they are rolled out is a vital way of managing the investment conflict.

A Shared Ambition

Unsuccessful organizations often try to resolve the communications conflict by strong-arming both businesses into creating a single message that functions for all contexts. Remember, one business's message relies on credibility, while the fundraising department's message relies on empathy. These are not similar foundations. The only way you can create a single message from these disparate aims is by compromising one or the other, and if you do that, you are either going to damage your organization's credibility or your organization's income or both. Neither of these outcomes is desirable.

Great Fundraising Organizations manage the communications conflict by acknowledging that it cannot be resolved. Both businesses need different messages because they are speaking to different customers with different needs.

Hang on, you say. *How can you have two different messages in an organization? What about cohesion and internal harmony? What about working toward a common goal?*

Well, I'm glad you asked. What both businesses must do is anchor on a shared purpose. This is the purpose of the organization at the highest level, rearticulated for the current climate; this has to be singular, unified, and clear. Once both businesses have that shared purpose, they can create different messages based on it: one for credibility and one for fundraising.

What Can You Do?

As a fundraising director, most of the solutions in this chapter may feel out of your hands. You may feel like you don't have the power to create institutional change in your organization or implement these insights. I get it; a lot of these decisions rest with the senior leadership and the board and the direction they choose to take the organization in.

But power does, in fact, lie in your hands. Now that you have understood that you're running a separate business within the non-profit, your job is to step up as a leader. You must take on the responsibility of being an internal advocate for the donor. If you don't do it, no one else will. Network within your organization; make time for face-to-face meetings, drink that coffee, and share that lunch so that you can represent your donors in informal as well as formal settings. Learn to lead upward; educate and direct your senior leadership and board about the changes they need to make in the organization to allow fundraising to succeed at the next level. This is what great fundraising leaders do: they spend 50% of their time fundraising and the other 50% teaching their organization how to best meet the needs of their donors.

Illustration: Royal Flying Doctor Service, Victoria, Australia

The Royal Flying Doctors Service, Victoria, Australia, was one of the first few dozen organizations we worked with after we had studied the academic dataset and were implementing our insights from the casework. Scott Chapman, the CEO, and his director of fundraising, Jacquie, were part of a group of 12 people who came from Melbourne to Amsterdam to attend an international fundraising congress. Then they flew over the next week to do a masterclass with us in the highlands of Scotland.

Several months later, I was in Australia, and they invited me to host a multiday seminar for their entire headquarters team and representatives of their board. Their pain point was simple: they felt like they were underperforming with regard to their organizational income as compared to the size of their brand. They were correct: they were pulling in a fairly modest revenue compared to their globally recognized name.

It was a great week. These were driven, high-performing individuals who were amazing to work with, and I took them through much of the content you'll be reading in the following chapters. But what really brought them to life was the insight of "two businesses, one mission." It was like it was a key they had been missing. From that moment onward, they changed.

At the end of the week, the chair of the board thanked me for my time. Then he announced to the room, "From now on, we are going to be as good in the business of fundraising as we have always been in the business of being flying doctors."

This was in 2015, so it was the early days of our program. I'll be honest with you: we were still testing our insights, so I had no real preconception of how big our discoveries would be. How could I? We were only in year one of results. But I got a glimpse of what was possible, of what we were achieving, when the chair of that board stood up and made his announcement. This was a senior, experienced leader who had looked at our dataset and our analysis and had discovered a whole new layer of growth.

Maybe, just maybe, we were on to something big. Maybe, just maybe, we had created something valuable.

The Royal Flying Doctors Service was true to their word; they restructured their operations so that their fundraising department had the freedom and materials to function as a separate business that met the needs of their donors. Marie Quirke became head of the fundraising team, and the organization has taken their total revenue from $17 million to over $80 million over seven years, including fundraising growth, government funding, and commercial contracts.

The fundraising growth contributing to this is a transformational 136% – tens of millions of dollars. (If you are wondering where Jacqui's story went, she decided to move to another organization to ensure integrity when she and Scott realized they were in love. They are now married – a real happy ending.)

Two Businesses, One Mission

Royal Flying Doctor Service Victoria

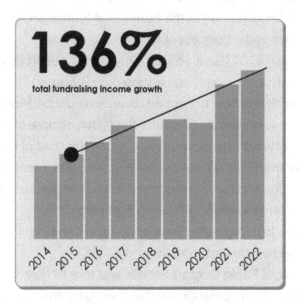

Figure 1.8 Royal Flying Doctors Service growth chart.
Source: Revolutionise International Limited 2024.

Key Takeaways

As Heath McSolvin stumbled upon that day, each charity is, in fact, two businesses with one mission. We should stop torturing ourselves attempting the key integration of these two businesses. Instead, like the Great Fundraising Organizations, we should focus on being the best at both.

To do this, the top-level leaders must accept both businesses as distinct and must commit to being as good at meeting the needs of their donors as they are at meeting the needs of their service users. This means prioritizing investment as appropriate

---

to drive required growth, recognizing that the culture and functions of the fundraising department differ from the rest of the organization, and creating powerful communications required to deliver rapid and sustainable fundraising growth.

Consultations, involvement, and education should be widespread across the nonprofit, but it is key that these decisions are then made by leadership before filtering down. Moreover, this top-level decision-making should be made without compromise, and the board and chief executives should be willing to stick by it.

If your charity is able to do this, then you've set the foundation of a Great Fundraising Organization. You are one step closer to triggering the Red Dot.

Chapter 2

From Governance to Growth

The Trifecta

A Red Dot moment is an incredible phenomenon. It looks like a simple point on a graph, but it symbolizes the beginning of a large surge of growth that redefines what an organization is capable of. The lead-up to the Red Dot is equally special. It is as if decades-old organizations have turned into start-ups again; they become focused and energized, and they rediscover their drive. But what creates this transformation? How does a flatlining organization revitalize itself to trigger unprecedented growth?

In 2012, my business partner at the time, Ken Burnett, and I had the pleasure of seeing Guide Dogs undergo this transformation first-hand. On the day it happened, we were in the room.

At the time, the Guide Dogs for the Blind Association had been around for 80 years but had flatlined in terms of income. Don't get me wrong, it wasn't in crisis. It had a large sustainable income from legacy funding and a modest individual giving program, which was enough to run a balanced budget year-on-year and generate a small surplus. Still, they had had no noticeable growth; they were subsisting.

Jayne George, their director of fundraising, had managed to convince the board to convene a special meeting on fundraising. This was at a board retreat, and she had invited Ken and me along. We knew how special this meeting was; it was an unusual luxury for a board to set aside a whole day to discuss fundraising, which was an often-ignored topic, and Jayne had lobbied hard to make it happen.

The chairman of Guide Dogs was John Stewart. He was a senior banking executive; he served as chairman of Legal & General, a British asset management company, as well as a nonexecutive director of the Finance Reporting Council.

John was not satisfied with subsisting.

He opened the board meeting with the most spectacular line. I still remember it; we were all sitting around the long table, chatting, bubbly, looking at the formal agenda for the day. There was John, walking in and taking his seat at the head of the table, politely calling the meeting to order. The chatter died down, heads turned, and then we were all looking at him, waiting for his next words. I don't know what we thought it would be – probably a reading of the agenda or perhaps a restating of the usual budgetary needs for the coming financial year. We certainly didn't expect what came next.

"Ladies and gentlemen," John said, "there are 180,000 people in the United Kingdom who cannot leave their homes because they are losing their sight. The purpose of this meeting is to solve that problem."

There was a surprised silence. A couple of people exchanged looks. Was John serious? Surely not. Someone guffawed, and it was as if they had broken the ice; the humor spread, and there were titters and laughs along the table.

"That's a big challenge, John," someone said wryly. "It's going to take a lot of time."

Someone else quipped, "Not to mention an awful lot of money." More laughter.

John waited patiently for people to settle down. Of course it would take time and money – especially money, which is why they'd come together today to discuss fundraising. Guide Dogs needed to expand their capacity if they were going to reach 180,000 people.

Here's what John had done with that spectacular first line: he had stated a problem that the nonprofit had to solve across the long-term. It could be in the next 5 years or 7 years or 10 years, but it was definitely in the long-term; no one was going to reach thousands of people by the next financial year. By doing so, John had made that problem the objective of fundraising. No one was asking, *How do we cautiously manage our organization?* or *How do we retain a modest surplus next year?* Instead, they were thinking, *How on earth do we reach 180,000 who are losing their eyesight and cannot leave their homes?*

It was fascinating to see the impact of that objective ripple across the boardroom. There was some polite but direct challenge to John's statement. The board members were intelligent people who could see that it would be a monumental task to achieve what John was asking. It might even be unfeasible. Why set it as their goal? Why reach so far you are almost guaranteed to fail?

So John told a story.

Years ago, he had a friend at the bank who fell ill. As a result of the illness, this friend began to lose his eyesight in his 40s. It was sudden, it was unexpected, and there was no ready help available. His friend was too proud to go looking for assistance. He kept living life as normal, pretending his eyesight was just fine, even as it deteriorated. Then one day, he woke up and it was gone.

The friend tried to keep working but couldn't, so he lost his job. He retreated into himself. His wife tried to help him, but he pushed her away until she was unable to cope. She left. He became a stranger to his children. He stopped leaving the house. He took to drinking, wrapped deep in his own despair. He rarely met anyone, rarely spoke to anyone. He started to drink very heavily, and eventually, he died.

"If help had been available for him," John said, "my friend would still have his job, his family, and his life. Each of those 180,000 people could be my friend. Who do you suggest we don't save?"

After that, there was no debate about whether 180,000 people were too many. Instead, I watched as an organization galvanized themselves around an ambitious, powerful goal; they stopped trying to change the problem and instead focused on solving it. Giving 180,000 people a guide dog was unfeasible; there weren't enough guide dogs, and it was not always the most appropriate solution. Should the nonprofit pivot to fixing eyesight loss? But there was already another organization that tackled this problem; Guide Dogs was a mobility organization, so it made sense to focus their solutions on mobility.

Ultimately, the board settled on a simple description of the three things that their nonprofit could do to help people with failing eyesight stay mobile, which could be simply communicated to donors:

- Provide a guide dog
- Get a person to assist them
- Offer them technology that could help

The board decided that all 180,000 people must be able to get whichever combination of these solutions that would allow them to live a full and productive life.

Once they identified how to solve this problem, the board then spent the next seven hours trying to identify the decisions they needed to make to effectively implement these solutions. The key, they realized, was investment in fundraising. The trustees decided to withdraw part of the money from the nonprofit's significant reserves and invest it in fundraising growth. As the treasurer told Jayne when the board meeting ended, "We've been working on this all day, and I am now of the opinion that we're not investing enough under the current fundraising proposals."

One day, one meeting (although, admittedly, a very long meeting). It unlocked compound growth for Guide Dogs. Over a period of eight years, the team at Guide Dogs drove their voluntary income from £54 million to £109 million. More importantly, the number of people their service could reach accelerated at a faster rate than their income after the first 18 months of investment started to show a return.

It all began at that meeting. If you look at the chart of their revenue before and after that meeting, you can see it clearly – they triggered the Red Dot.

So what happened on that day that helped trigger the Red Dot? In a very short span of time, John, their chairman, stated a problem that became the new ambition of the organization: to reach 180,000 people who were losing their eyesight, were unable to leave their homes, and were not getting the services of Guide Dogs. Second, there was a distinct cultural change across the board when John told his friend's story. The mindset shifted from *How do we fund the running costs of our organization?* to *How do we solve a long-term problem?* It would take months, of course, for the cultural change to permeate throughout the whole organization, but the top-level leadership had been transformed that day. And third, they committed significant investment toward fundraising growth.

This is what we call the Trifecta of great fundraising preparedness, the three elements that must be in place to kickstart a surge of growth:

- New ambition: A big, external idea that unifies the organization and ensures they're working toward solving a common problem
- Culture shift: The whole nonprofit becomes aligned and values fundraising and the donors as much as they do their service users and their projects
- Investment plan: A financial plan that invests in fundraising over the long-term

51

Guide Dogs

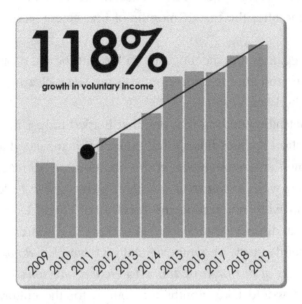

Figure 2.1 Guide Dogs growth chart.
Source: Revolutionise International Limited 2024.

These are the three biggest building blocks of a Great Fundraising Organization, placed on top of the foundation of "two businesses, one mission." You'll notice that each of the Trifecta links directly to the three conflicts we discussed in Chapter 1. The new ambition solves the communications conflict, the cultural shift accounts for the cultural conflict, and the investment plan addresses the investment conflict. We'll dive more into how the Trifecta draws upon and resolves the tensions of the three conflicts in the coming chapters, but for now, think of it as a house. The concept of "two businesses in one" is the foundation, the groundwork on which all growth is based. Upon that foundation, you place the cornerstones of the Trifecta, which are the building blocks of a Great Fundraising Organization.

We discovered the Trifecta by studying the best of the best. The Great Fundraising Organizations in our initial research dataset arrived at this Trifecta intuitively, and it is what distinguished them from the vast majority of organizations that were floundering. Interestingly, we found that successful nonprofits always had all three strands of the Trifecta, as opposed to only one or two.

The data is overwhelmingly clear: to create a surge of growth and trigger a Red Dot moment, your two businesses must be aligned on all three elements of the Trifecta – a new ambition, a cultural shift, and an investment plan.

The Trifecta Is a Leadership Issue

Agreeing and committing to this Trifecta is a leadership issue.

What do we mean by a "leadership issue"? We mean that "leadership" is distinct from "management," which can roughly be traced to two aspects:

- Who is making these decisions?
- What are the quality and focus of these decisions?

The Trifecta cannot be decided only by middle management. These are not tasks or projects that can be delegated to managers for further analysis, endless feasibility studies, or circuitous discussions. To implement the Trifecta at a nonprofit, it has to be decided and committed to at the very highest level of leadership, and then it has to be consistently adhered to so as to create sustainable, long-term growth.

Think back to Guide Dogs. That meeting created phenomenal change, but it did so because it was a board meeting; the highest decision-makers of the organization were present and aligned. If the chairman hadn't been the person providing the problem to solve, the vision may not have been as persuasive. If the board hadn't agreed to be persuaded and change how they culturally approached their responsibilities, there would have been no impetus to rethink how they ran the nonprofit. And if the board had not used that cultural shift to free up money for fundraising investment, Guide Dogs may not have seen such a huge surge in revenue growth.

But because it was a board meeting and everyone in that room had the power to execute and action change, the decisions taken during that day transformed the fate of the organization. A very similar meeting, for example, of a manager sharing the same story with their team over lunch may not have been as powerful. Perhaps it would have galvanized the team, but it could not have reshaped the nonprofit's trajectory.

This is not to say, of course, that only the board and chief executives have power. Think about Jayne George, the director of fundraising at Guide Dogs. The board meeting would never have taken place without her insistence and lobbying. Indeed, she worked closely with John Stewart before the meeting to help him see what fundraising growth could do for the organization. In short, she did what all great fundraising leaders do: she led upward.

But for the Trifecta to be effective, it has to be decided and committed to (without compromise) at top-level leadership before those decisions are communicated downward and implemented throughout the nonprofit.

Leadership also differs from management in terms of the quality and focus of their decision-making. Management's job is to handle a business's day-to-day operations: it is involved with the short-term, the logistics, and the operations. To do their jobs well, middle management must be detail-oriented and pay close attention to the nitty-gritty.

Leadership, on the other hand, can be defined by three criteria.

Think Big Picture

If management is focused on details, then leadership looks to the big picture. This means that leaders have to act with the long-term in mind and create a vision for the organization that stretches across a larger time horizon.

Focus on Leading People

If management is occupied with logistics and systems, particularly with ensuring that a business functions smoothly in the day to day, then leadership's job is to focus on people. As we saw in Chapter 1, the three conflicts are essentially people issues; they stem from conflicts between how people act, identify, believe, and behave. Leadership is responsible for tackling the root of these issues so that people are motivated and aligned to give their best.

Live with Uncertainty

The biggest quality that distinguishes leaders from management is a leader's ability to live with uncertainty. Think of it this way: to be a good leader, you have to be fiercely pragmatic about where you are now and absolutely idealistic about where you want to go. These two points – where you are now and where you are going – never change, but you must be flexible in how you get from this pragmatic present to the idealistic future.

With Guide Dogs, the pragmatic present was that 180,000 people couldn't leave their homes because they were blind. This was a fact. The ideal future they were working toward was that each of those people must live a new, full life. The job of the board was to create a metaphorical bridge between that present and that future. However, it was not possible for them to plan every paving stone in that bridge. All they could do was plan in big spans and trust that their team would fill in the gaps when the time came.

I've never seen a plan go straight from A to B, not once. Data changes, markets change, personnel leave, the world shifts onto a new axis. The job of a leader is not to fix the details of a plan and then stick to it no matter what. It is to set the destination and then adapt to the curveballs the world sends along the way.

So what does this mean for the Trifecta and how it should be approached? It means that the three strands – investment, culture, and the new ambition – should not be seen as detailed plans but rather as aims that the leadership commits to fulfilling. A leader should accept that these aims will need to be refreshed at some point, and that there will be consistent tension in the details, but that each strand must be committed to without compromise. In other words, a leader accepts that their destination is a fixed point – it never changes – but that there are many different roads to get there.

Shifting Mindsets: From Governance to Growth

To approach the Trifecta correctly, one must begin by defining the problem one needs to solve in the next 5–10 years and then work backward to see what kind of investment and decisions one must make now to solve that problem. But to do this, an organization's leadership needs to shift from a governance mindset to a growth mindset.

In organizations that stagnate, the board usually only adopts a governance mindset. This means that their sole aim is to run the organization in the most efficient manner possible, which means holding their operations up to scrutiny and accountability. More often than not, this translates into controlling the finances of the organization. If your sole aim is to run a stable nonprofit, then it is natural to ensure that the nonprofit spends as little as possible so that you consistently have a balanced budget (and hopefully a surplus of revenue).

A governance view is essential. It is indeed the board's responsibility to exercise a degree of control over the nonprofit and guide it so that it remains sustainable. Yet, in the Great Fundraising Organizations, the boards move beyond this role of governance toward one of growth. Their focus is not just on creating a well-run organization but on solving a long-term problem. As a result, their financial approach is not to spend as little money as possible but to spend as much money as possible to fulfill this goal.

This shift is very noticeable in our Guide Dogs story. Before the board meeting, Guide Dogs had operated with a pure governance mindset; they focused on how much money they required to run the nonprofit from one year to the next, and they kept a tight budget. As a result, they were operational, but their growth had flatlined.

After the board meeting, they changed to a growth mindset. Their goal now was to help the 180,000 people stuck at home who were losing their eyesight, and the board was willing to invest whatever it took to solve that problem. As a result, they accelerated exponential growth.

It is not easy for top-tier leadership to shift from a governance mindset to a growth mindset. All boards have a legal mandate for good governance, but there is no legal mandate for good growth. It has to be an active choice on the part of the leadership; are they here to manage a nonprofit, or are they here to solve a problem? If they choose the former, they will be fulfilling their responsibilities, but they will also be choosing fundraising stagnation. If they choose the latter, it creates a cultural shift that reverberates throughout the organization and pulls everyone into alignment.

For here is the truth: no professional fundraiser joined a nonprofit to help balance a budget. They joined to make the world a better place. Similarly, no donor gives money to a charity so that the charity can maintain a good balance sheet. They give so that they can make someone's life better. If you want money to manage an organization and the donor wants to solve a problem, you are incongruent. But if you are all aligned on solving a problem, then everyone progresses with renewed purpose and energy.

In our early datasets, the Great Fundraising Organizations chose a growth mindset intuitively. They decided the problem they wanted to solve in the long-term and then worked backward to see what needed to be done in the present (particularly in terms of investment) to achieve their goals. A famous example is a spectacular, fast-growing organization in the United States called the Wounded Warrior Project. Their founding board had skilled fundraisers on it, and so when they chose the name of the nonprofit, they made sure it reflected the charity's purpose. "Wounded" is the problem they are trying to solve, and "warrior" is their emotional differentiation from other organizations. Their purpose is baked into their name, visible right there every day to anchor them.

And it drives them. They are famous for very fast and very sustainable fundraising growth. Noticeably, they had a big public relations disaster a few years ago, but it was only a blip in their growth record because their fundraising and organizational purpose carried them through. Today, they are still one of the greatest fundraising organizations.

Another famous example is the National Society for the Prevention of Cruelty to Children (NSPCC), which was part of the first group of organizations we studied; it was led at the time by the aforementioned Giles Pegram. One of NSPCC's most popular campaigns was the "Full Stop" appeal, which set out to raise £250 million over a seven-year period – five times their annual revenue of about £50 million.

How on earth did they manage to set such an audacious goal? Like all successful organizations, they began by asking themselves, *What problem are we trying to solve?* The first iteration of the problem was simple: *We are here to eliminate the sexual, emotional, and physical abuse of children in the United Kingdom.*

There was immediate pushback within the organization. It was impossible to eliminate child abuse entirely, and so to set that as a goal meant losing their credibility. They could say they wanted to reduce child abuse but not eliminate it.

That led to a discussion: by how much should they reduce it? It did not take long for the people involved in that discussion to realize that they were trying to agree on the appropriate level of child abuse. There was no appropriate level of child abuse. It was simply wrong. So whether it was possible or not, the only realistic and morally correct goal they could set was to eliminate child abuse entirely. Thus, the "Full Stop" campaign was born: "Cruelty to children must stop. FULL STOP." When Giles introduced this to groups of donors and prospective donors, 100% of them agreed this was the right aspiration for the NSPCC, and 100% also agreed it was impossible (don't worry, we will explain this seeming contradiction in Chapter 4).

By setting a long-term goal and working back from it, NSPCC was able to set an audacious financial target – and achieve it. They exceeded that £250 million total in seven years. Not only that, but they also increased their sustainable revenue by 360%, from £50 million to £180 million.

Both examples show how powerful a growth mindset can be. In the case of the Wounded Warriors, they put the problem they were trying to solve into their name as a permanent reminder; it focused, guided, and drove the organization. In the case of the NSPCC, identifying the problem – no matter how audacious – and working backward to achieve it created a deliberate surge of fundraising growth at a colossal scale.

Illustration: Feenix, Cape Town, South Africa

I first met Nyasha Njela at the masterclass I did in Stellenbosch, South Africa, in 2017. It was a great session: I had planned for 12 people and about 200 showed up, so I ended up speaking at a large lecture hall in the University of Stellenbosch, with people sitting on the steps in between rows and all of us having a great time. Nyasha was right in the front seat; I remember her because she was taking detailed notes of every one of our research findings.

Soon after the masterclass, Nyasha transitioned into a new role as a head of fundraising for a South African nonprofit, Feenix. Feenix was a start-up that was focused on helping people gain access to education; they funded students who couldn't otherwise afford university. When Nyasha joined, the nonprofit was finding their legs and looking to grow.

The moment she joined Feenix, Nyasha executed the Trifecta and building blocks from A to Z. She started by honing in on the problem they wanted to solve to make sure it was as precise as possible. Cross-departmental teams workshopped this and landed on "Education should not be dependent on wealth." It was a brilliant new ambition because firstly, it was personal. Nyasha was forced to drop out of university after her first year because her parents ran out of money.

Secondly, it was also the story of a nation. The big problem in South Africa is inherited wealth and privilege; how do you break that cycle? The only way to do that on a sustainable basis is education. But, at the time, education in South Africa was dependent

Feenix

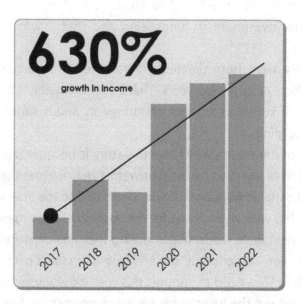

630%
growth in income

2017 2018 2019 2020 2021 2022

Figure 2.2 Feenix growth chart.
Source: Revolutionise International Limited 2024.

on wealth; only the rich could afford it, which made the problem permanent. Feenix's new ambition spoke right to the core of the issue; if it was solved, it benefited the individual but it also benefited the nation.

In terms of culture, Feenix made the decision that they would be as good at fundraising as they were at helping disadvantaged students. They put fundraising right up there in their mission statement. They shut the office twice every year so that all the staff members can attend online conferences on fundraising, including the nonfundraisers. Even the students applying for Feenix support are trained in fundraising so they can participate in their own success.

(continued)

(continued)

For investment, Nyasha and the CEO, Leana de Beer, worked continuously with the board to ensure they had the optimum long-term investment in fundraising and that it was reviewed quarterly.

Feenix went from practically zero revenue to a cumulative 176 million rand in five years. That's approximately $9 million, which is a stunning amount of money in South Africa. It was mind-boggling.

Part of the reason why I love this story is because it is a great illustration of how you can lead upward. I've since met the CEO of Feenix, Leana de Beer, and she has described to me how vital her relationship with Nyasha was for the success of the organization. It was a deliberate leadership coupling that was consciously created. As Leana describes it, she and Nyasha made a pact. Nyasha said to her, "You need to support this methodology, manage the board, and get the investment I need to protect my fundraising team from interference." And Leana said to her, "I've got your back. I trust you to get us the money we need to make Feenix grow."

Alignment accelerates growth to stratospheric levels.

Key Takeaways

To trigger the Red Dot, your two businesses must be aligned on the three elements: the new ambition, a cultural shift, and an investment plan. This is the Trifecta of great fundraising preparedness, and they form the cornerstones of a Great Fundraising Organization.

Remember that the Trifecta is a leadership issue. This means the three elements do not exist in the everyday or in the details but rather in broad strokes, with a focus on the big picture and the long-term. The Trifecta can only be decided upon by top-tier leadership, who must commit to these three strands without compromise and then drive this change throughout the nonprofit. The leadership must be able to adapt to changing circumstances, live with uncertainty, and implement the Trifecta without modifying the goal or changing the destination. The trick is to be pragmatic about the present, idealistic about the future, and flexible in how you get from one to the other.

The leadership must also transition from a governance mindset to a growth mindset. In a governance framework, the aim is to manage the nonprofit from one financial year to the next and thus spend as little money as possible to ensure a balanced spreadsheet. In a growth framework, the focus is very clearly on the problem the organization wants to solve in the next 10 years and on spending as much money as possible to solve that problem.

Switching from a governance mindset to a growth mindset is a choice. It is an audacious and ambitious choice, but it is also necessary. For once you choose a growth mindset, you create alignment between the organization, your staff, your donors, and your service users. And alignment, as we've seen, propels you toward success.

A Great Fundraising Organization is not something you do. It is something you are.

Chapter 3

Alignment Begins with the New Ambition

When we first commissioned the original research on the Great Fundraising Organizations, Professors Sargeant and Shang and their team came back with a key observation:

The greatest block to fundraising is internal conflict leading to consensus-seeking compromise.

We didn't believe it. Surely it couldn't be the biggest block? We pushed back, but the research team was adamant that this is what the data revealed. So we tested it, and all our casework since then has proven it to be true. The biggest block to great fundraising is internal conflict. The best solution is alignment.

WWF is one of the world's leading nonprofits on conservation. Most of us will have heard of WWF; their logo of a black and white panda is almost universally recognizable. WWF historically built its fundraising on a simple technique: a donor was asked to sponsor species that were endangered or close to extinction, such as a panda or a tiger. The beauty of this fundraising device was that the donor felt immediately involved: they knew exactly where their money was going (to save a particular species), and they felt like they were helping in concrete ways. There was a clear connection between giving and making a difference.

Gradually, however, WWF had to go through an internal evolution. The world around them had changed, so to match it, they changed their internal structures and priorities. Climate change had emerged as the core issue over the last 20 years, and their major priority became tackling climate change, as well as what we could do as consumers to reverse it.

This created a systemic conflict. The fundraising department found themselves in an environment where it was difficult to thrive. WWF was known for saving animals, but now the conservation department needed to focus on climate change as opposed to individual species. The tenor of the messaging to the public changed as well: it veered closer toward educating the public than coopting them into a shared desire to save animals. Plus, there were already several organizations dedicated to solving climate change. Why would a donor pick WWF to give their money to instead of another organization known for battling the climate crisis? What on earth made WWF different? And if nothing made WWF different, how was the fundraising department supposed to recruit donors?

In extreme moments, the internal conflict radiated outward to its many satellite charities in various countries. When no one could agree on what to focus on, no one could sign off on communications without much debate and eventual compromise.

WWF in Norway reached out to us to resolve this problem with them. What we discovered over the course of several days and many conversations was that WWF's unique selling point would always be their specialization in flora and fauna, particularly the focus on animals. This was what they were known for. Thus, in order to distinguish themselves from other nonprofits battling climate change, they had to focus on the natural world as a differentiator. But how do you do that and account for the conservation department's emphasis on the climate crisis?

The gap, we realized, was merely a change in scale. The problem that WWF Norway was trying to solve before climate change emerged was "some of the animals are dying." Now, thanks to the climate crisis, it was "all of the animals are dying."

That's it; three days in a room, and we changed four letters. It became WWF Norway's new ambition, a focus that essentially said, *Look, the problem is the same. It just got larger.* It created an immediate and sustained increase in their income because now the donor understood the urgency behind WWF's appeal; they saw what differentiated WWF from other nonprofits and where their money was going.

Five years later, WWF Norway refreshed their new ambition again to create a new fundraising surge. Their purpose was still the same – to save all species from extinction – but they reworked it to make it more immediate and personalized. What they ended up with was:

"Redd all natur nå. For alle. For alltid."
In English, this translates into "Save all nature now. For everyone. Forever."

The message was extremely simple: we need to reverse climate change because if we don't, all of nature is going to die. It addresses the conservation department's emphasis on the climate crisis, but it keeps the focus on nature that the fundraising team needs to recruit donors and grow the nonprofit's income. It was a new ambition that both businesses of the nonprofit could get behind.

Based on this second shared ambition, WWF Norway ran a series of fundraising messages that were instantly emotive. They could now include people too because humans are, after all, part of nature. We could be saving nature for Erik, a child who wants to see the tigers and cannot because they are nearly extinct. This is our Earth. Saving it means saving all life.

WWF Norway

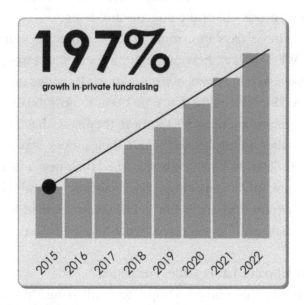

Figure 3.1 WWF Norway growth chart.
Source: Revolutionise International Limited 2024.

WWF Norway, with fundraising led throughout by Ina Toften, have now trebled their donor income while at all times maintaining integrity around a simple truth: climate change has made the problem much bigger and more urgent.

The very first stage of growing fundraising income is internal alignment. Without internal alignment, your organization remains paralyzed – or everyone compromises to create a solution that no one is happy with. But if you create real alignment, you create a driving force that is far more powerful than anything you can do externally. WWF Norway was stuck because the different departments could not agree on how to communicate their focus. Once they found the common goal that aligned their two businesses – and did so without compromise – they freed themselves to accelerate.

So how do you create internal alignment? You begin with the first part of the Trifecta: the new ambition.

Cascading Effect

Our casework shows that internal alignment is so powerful because it focuses the Great Fundraising Organizations. Without alignment, time and resources are wasted on choosing a direction and on arguing about what that direction should be. But with alignment, everyone is on the same page, which means a nonprofit can streamline and direct its resources toward a common goal.

Internal alignment begins with the new ambition because it *is* that common goal. A simple definition of the new ambition, that first block of the Trifecta, is it is a precise problem you are trying to solve in the next 5–10 years. For WWF Norway, "all the animals are dying" became a simple rallying cry that its two businesses could get behind.

Think of the classic definition of a "team:" people with different skill sets cooperating to achieve a shared goal. If everyone in your organization is working toward the new ambition, their collective efforts line up to build on each other, and you multiply impact. But if there is no shared ambition to rally around, then their efforts diffuse or cannibalize each other, and your organization remains stuck.

This is why the new ambition is the first step of the Trifecta on your road to triggering the Red Dot. It creates a cascading effect. According to our casework, if we start with the new ambition and multiple representatives of the two businesses are involved in defining and owning that ambition, then it goes a long way toward resolving the cultural conflict almost automatically. It is as if creating that new ambition reminds everyone that they are a team: they all have different skills, but each of those skills is required to reach that goal. Cultural comradery becomes a by-product.

Once the board buys into the new ambition and the culture of the organization starts to align behind it, then the board is much more likely to look favorably on an investment plan that stretches into the long-term. This happens for two reasons. First, the new ambition has helped the board recognize the need for more money. By design, a new ambition is an audacious goal, so it requires more revenue to achieve it. Second, if the ambition is in place and the culture is in alignment, the board has an enhanced level of confidence that the financial proposal is viable and will yield results. It is as simple as that.

We've seen this play out clearly with Guide Dogs, which we covered in Chapter 2. We can see it in WWF as well: the conservation department and the fundraising department only stopped fighting once they found a new ambition that addressed both of their needs.

Our big lesson from this is to start with the new ambition because it immediately forces the organization to think in the long-term as opposed to thinking about next year's budget, and it creates internal alignment. It also coaxes the culture into alignment because this alignment is necessary for all stakeholders to agree on a new ambition. And if the ambition and the culture are in place, you will have a board that is a lot more favorable to an audacious financial proposal.

Communications Hierarchy

To understand the role of a new ambition in an organization's success, it is necessary to see how it relates to the communications of a nonprofit as a whole.

Figure 3.2 is what we call the communications hierarchy of a Great Fundraising Organization. Right at the top is an organization's purpose. Think of this as the reason why the nonprofit was founded in the first place, the holistic mission it hopes to achieve in the world. A good purpose (i.e. a purpose that is well articulated) not only

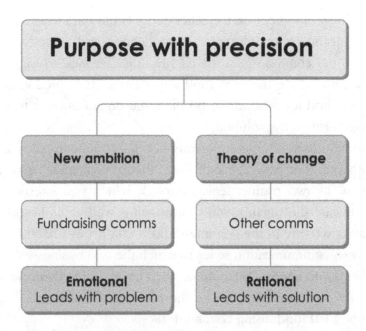

Figure 3.2 Communications hierarchy.
Source: Revolutionise International Limited 2024.

creates a cohesive identity within an organization but also differentiates the nonprofit from other businesses. In other words, a good purpose is precise so that it attracts the right people to the charity and clarifies the organization's unique selling point from other charities.

From that top level of "purpose with precision" hangs two strands of communication within an organization: theory of change and the new ambition.

Recall in Chapter 1 that we talked about the two businesses within your nonprofit and their two different communication needs, which create the communications conflict. We are now putting names to those two communication styles. "Theory of change" is the style and core of all nonfundraising communications within an organization. These are predominantly rational communications designed to build the credibility of the organization, as well as evidence of the quality of the organization's work.

Alignment Begins with the New Ambition

The new ambition, on the other hand, is the big idea that drives all fundraising communications. Once defined and agreed upon, it becomes the common goal the charity unites around to trigger the Red Dot and drive the next fundraising surge. It is predominantly emotional and focuses on the problem the organization is trying to solve rather than the solution.

We will discuss the components of a good new ambition in the next chapter. For now, think of both "theory of change" and "new ambition" as two distinct lenses through which you interpret and communicate the organization's purpose (as well as its history and work). As we saw in the communications conflict in Chapter 1, you need both communication styles to match the two businesses' different clients and needs. Organizations that try to merge them can only do so by compromising one or the other, and compromise is the death of great fundraising communications.

Purpose Versus New Ambition

It is relatively easy to distinguish between theory of change and a new ambition, but it is not always as easy to draw the line between a charity's purpose and their new ambition. After all, both address the problem the charity wants to tackle in the world, and they communicate the change the nonprofit hopes to create.

But a nonprofit's purpose and the new ambition are distinct. An organization's purpose is permanent; it is the reason why the charity was founded. The fundraising new ambition, on the other hand, is the problem the organization is trying to solve within the next 5–10 years for which they require more money. The new ambition is derived from the purpose, and it must define a common goal that moves the charity closer toward achieving the purpose, but it is not the same as the purpose. Nor is it permanent; once the new ambition has been achieved (or, more commonly, not achieved) across a

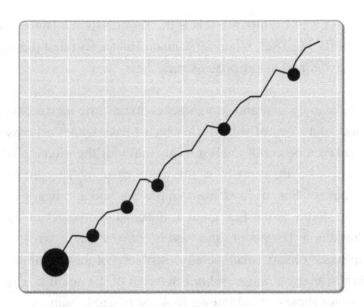

Figure 3.3 Triggering multiple Red Dots.
Source: Revolutionise International Limited 2024.

10-year period, the organization agrees on and aligns behind another ambition so that it can implement the Trifecta again and trigger the next fundraising surge.

Nothing in business is absolute, of course, and there are exceptions to every rule. There are cases where the charity's new ambition is the same as their purpose, but this is only for the duration of a surge. Once the surge plateaus, the charity must pick a different ambition to keep accelerating toward growth.

The first question we asked ourselves when we saw the dataset is *Why do Great Fundraising Organizations create new ambitions?* Why not simply make the purpose their common goal and use that to create internal alignment that drives fundraising growth?

We discovered two reasons. The first is because while purpose is permanent, times change. To reflect those changing times, you need a new ambition that refreshes every 5–10 years.

Alignment Begins with the New Ambition

An excellent example of this is the Royal National Lifeboat Institution (RNLI). In 1823, when Sir William Hillary founded the organization, he defined its purpose as such:

> For many years, and in various countries, the melancholy and fatal cases of shipwreck which I have witnessed have excited a powerful interest in my mind for the situation of those who are exposed to this awful calamity. The preservation of human lives from shipwreck should always be considered as the first great and permanent object of the institution. The people and vessels of every nation, whether in peace or war, [shall] be equally objects of this institution, whilst every stranger, whom disasters of the sea may cast on her shores, should never look for refuge in vain.

This is elaborate and flowery language, but it was perfect for Sir William's Victorian audience. Today, the RNLI articulates its purpose in one sentence: "Save all lives at sea." The purpose is the same, but it is a lot shorter to reflect the modern world.

The RNLI has been fundraising now for more than 200 years, and every 5–6 years, they create a new ambition that reflects the world around them. Each of these new ambitions are fundraising variations of the purpose, and each of them brings the RNLI closer to their purpose while remaining distinct:

- "Come to the rescue too. Your contribution may save a life."
- "Lives depend on you, as much as on them."
- "Answer our call and we'll be able to answer yours."

Thus, purpose is permanent but times change, and the new ambition reflects those changing times. It must be constantly refreshed to stay relevant.

The second reason why Great Fundraising Organizations form new ambitions is because the process of creating a new ambition creates alignment, which is why it must be repeated every 5–10 years. Say an organization chooses an ambition in year 1, and then aligns their culture and finances behind it to trigger a Red Dot. After a period of growth, entropy settles in. People leave, and new members join the organization. These newcomers do not understand the shared ambition, as they haven't been part of creating it and do not emotionally own it. It then becomes harder for everyone to align because the ambition is not a common goal anymore; it does not belong to everyone. By year 10, the organization's focus has fuzzied again. The only way to kickstart a new fundraising surge is to choose a fresh ambition that gets everyone on the same page.

"We Have a Problem. You Can Help Solve It."

The mistake that organizations often make when creating a new ambition is that they focus on an internal problem instead of an external one. The theory of change communications focuses on an internally driven solution: they describe what the organization will achieve with the donor's money. But for the new ambition to work, it must do the opposite: it must describe what the donor will achieve by giving the money.

In other words, the theory of change communications is predominantly aimed at the service user and says, "You have a problem. We can help solve it." A new ambition must be aimed at the donor and say, "We have a problem. You can help solve it."

The Centre for Creative Education (CCE) in South Africa was struggling to find a new ambition that was inspiring enough to attract donors. Their work focuses on raising money to train teachers so that the teachers can provide creative education for marginalized children in South Africa. The problem they were looking to solve was "We need money to train teachers," which is important but not very compelling or differentiating as a new ambition.

75

Alignment Begins with the New Ambition

When we worked with them, they realized that there were two service users of their organization. The first was the teachers, but the second was the children themselves. These children were missing creativity from their education, and creativity is key to connection. The result was a whole generation that was disconnected from learning; ambition; fun; emotions; passions; culture; imagination; society; the past, present and future; nature; the environment; spirituality; and indeed, from each other.

Further, creative connection is critical to South Africa's development as a country. History is passed from generation to generation through stories, songs, and art. If the children do not learn these, they can't pass them on, and South Africa's diverse communities will lose their identities and heritage.

This was the problem CCE needed to solve. It was a massive breakthrough that led to their new ambition: "CCE will keep training teachers until every South African child can connect through creativity."

It was a perfect new ambition. It told the donor exactly what they could achieve by donating. It gave the fundraising team a powerful and audacious new problem that they could focus on to recruit new donors. Critically, it was emotive and unlocked emotive communications about both problem and solution. And it aligned the whole organization, because yes, the CCE's immediate internal problem was to fund teacher training, but the reason they wanted to fund teacher training was to solve the much bigger external problem of a disconnected generation.

Nonfundraising departments often believe they need to educate donors before donors will donate. In extreme cases, they see the donors as ignorant and good fundraising communications as teaching the donors a more moral way to live in a complicated world. But in actuality, it is much simpler than that. Donors just need to know there is a problem in the world they can help solve. Once everyone in your nonprofit understands and respects this, you unlock the route to the Red Dot.

Illustration: Children's Hospices Across Scotland, Scotland

In 2016, Children's Hospices Across Scotland (CHAS) was somewhat stagnant in terms of fundraising. There had been no growth in the organization for years, and they were running a small deficit. In the hope of turning things around, they brought in a new director, Iain McAndrew, with a mandate to transform fundraising income.

But CHAS had an endemic problem: there was a deep skepticism within the organization about their ability to raise money. I remember speaking to one person at the charity who said to me, "I don't see how we can raise much. Our work is in medical and social sciences. When you drill down, there's nothing very emotional about what we do."

I was flabbergasted. These were children's hospices. Every day, they opened their doors to give dying children the best end-of-life care. Every day, they spoke to and comforted parents who were facing a human being's worst nightmare. And here was someone who worked for them, genuinely telling me there was nothing emotional about what they did. Nothing emotional about a dying child? I remember saying to the person, gently, "Well, let's not drill down then. Let's stick to the big picture."

On one level, I can understand why CHAS had the problem it did. To run a children's hospice and deal with the grief they encountered every day, the people there had to have had years of training to manage their emotions. Otherwise, there was no way they could keep going. But what this had created was a professional culture that was deeply avoidant of emotions. I would go as far as to say they were scared of them.

(continued)

(continued)

So in 2016, CHAS called us in as part of a concurrent rebranding to rearticulate their purpose and create a new ambition. We started off with the same question as we always do: *What problem are you trying to solve now?*

This is not a simple question for children's hospice. CHAS knew that many of the children who came to them would die, so it was pointless to try and solve the terminal nature of the children's illnesses. We spent days on it until we finally hit upon one remarkable line that triggered everything else.

The problem that CHAS was trying to solve was *For every one of Scotland's unfortunate families, the final breath of their dying child should be as precious and memorable as the first.*

Every family remembers the first breath of their child. Only the most unfortunate families remember the last. But if, in that final breath, the mom and the dad can hold their child as they pass away; if in that breath they knew that their child had the best medical care, the best social care, the best friends, doctors, toys, education and environment; if they knew they had crammed as much joy as they could into their child's short life and that their child knew how deeply loved they were, now and forever, then the hospice would have achieved the best it could hope for.

CHAS started with that problem and worked with the families they serve. Together, they decided that the purpose of CHAS is to make the child's short life as joyful as possible and to make sure the families can remember the joy of that life and not only the tragedy of an early death. They reworked their purpose to "Keep the joy alive even in the face of death." This was shortened in credibility brand materials to "Keep the joy alive."

Once CHAS had their purpose, we looked for a specific external problem that the new ambition could focus on. How could

Great Fundraising Organizations

a donor help CHAS by donating? The organization realized that they were geographically limited: they could not reach every child and family in Scotland. At the time, they were only reaching one of every three families facing the tragedy of a dying child. If their purpose was to help families keep the joy alive across Scotland, then they needed more services, and they needed more fundraising income to do that.

So they rebranded. They changed their name from Children's Hospices Association Scotland to Children's Hospices Across Scotland. They created a new fundraising ambition that focused on their external problem: "No family should face the death of their child alone."

Since then, CHAS has increased their individual giving income by 757% (and it is still rising). Through a combination of expanded hospice provisions, local outreach services, and hospice-at-home services for the most remote areas, they now reach two out of every three families, as well as provide palliative support in hospitals across Scotland in partnership with the National Health Service.

Reaching alignment in this charity was hard. There was a lot of internal pushback and opinion that the public would not want to know about terminally ill children. They were hesitant to use the word "dying" and felt like the word "joy" was inappropriate.

This pushback continued until the organization again spoke to the families they represented. The parents' opinion was straightforward and unanimous. To them, this was their truth. Their child was dying; not saying it did not change that reality. It only hushed over what was a devastating tragedy that they had to live through. The families also said that their overwhelming takeaway from interaction with the hospices was joy.

(continued)

Alignment Begins with the New Ambition

(continued)

Children's Hospices Across Scotland

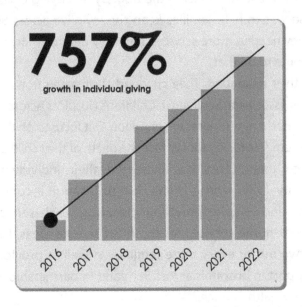

Figure 3.4 Children's Hospices Across Scotland growth chart.
Source: Revolutionise International Limited 2024.

After this, the doubters were persuaded that this was indeed the correct focus and the correct language, at which point the charity was able to achieve alignment.

Creating and maintaining internal alignment is a constant challenge. Sometimes you will find the right words and the right focus – that perfect new ambition – and the people within your organization will still disagree. As fundraising director, your job is not to compromise on the new ambition. It is to do whatever you can to help others see how this new articulation can create powerful change. It can be extremely hard to do, but put the effort in. It's absolutely worth it.

Key Takeaways

The number one block to great fundraising, according to the data, is internal conflict. The best solution is internal alignment.

Internal alignment is the start of every fundraising surge. You create internal alignment by creating a new ambition, a common goal that unites your two businesses and articulates a problem that you want to solve in the next 5–10 years. A new ambition must be agreed to by all the stakeholders in the organization without compromise; this means everyone should feel connected to it and have an emotional stake in it.

This is often hard to achieve. It may be an iterative process. It may involve resolving conflict by bringing the conflict out into the open, which can be uncomfortable. It may involve encouraging people to work in a difficult emotional space, a space they have spent their professional lives distancing themselves from. But keep going because it is worth it. It is what starts every fundraising surge, and therefore it is how you fulfill your purpose.

Remember that new ambitions should focus on an external problem, not an internal one. Don't focus on what the organization can achieve with the donor's money. Focus on what the donor can achieve by giving to you. If you do that, you will be able to create a new ambition that is compelling.

Lastly, you need a fresh new ambition (aligned with your permanent purpose) for every fundraising surge you do. This is because a new ambition is not eternal; it changes with the times, and it is designed to be achieved over a 10-year period. But it is also because the process of creating a new ambition, of agreeing

(continued)

Alignment Begins with the New Ambition

(continued)

on one, creates internal alignment, which is the start of everything. Sometimes, you may even need to refresh the communication of your purpose to reflect changing times and increased competition.

In the next chapter, let's look at the components of a good new ambition.

Chapter 4

Not Any Ambition Will Do

When Tina Hudgins invited me to work with International Justice Mission (IJM) in the United States, they were a relatively young organization – they were founded in 1997, so they didn't have centuries under their belt like some of the charities we work with. Still, they were already a good fundraising organization: they had an extremely professional, high-performing outfit and, thanks mainly to the contacts of their founder, had done particularly well with major donor philanthropists. The one place they were wrestling with was the mass marketing side of fundraising, where you engage lots of people. So they called us in.

The offices of IJM were based in Crystal City, Virginia, just on the outskirts of Washington, DC. You could see the Pentagon from their offices, which is always an interesting backdrop to a seminar series, especially for a Scot.

Those seminar series were full – a room of 80–90 people – and I talked them through much of what we are discussing in this book. When we came to the seminar on the new ambition, we hit an interesting problem.

Like most nongovernmental organizations, IJM was convinced it was impossible to narrow down what they do into a single ambition. They had about 100 projects around the world, each tackling different issues. How were they meant to shrink so many projects into one ambition? Simplicity was out of the question. Of course, I'd heard this before. Nonprofits love to describe the complexity of their projects and their variety.

"Look," I said, "let's give it a try."

So we broke into a detailed discussion about all of those projects, and through a combination of logical and emotional work, we narrowed them down to four big themes:

- People trafficking
- Bonded labor
- Sex trade
- The ambiguously named but ever-present category of "other"

We laughingly dismissed the last category immediately, so we were left with three big themes. How did we narrow it down from there? What connected these themes? If we discovered that, we could look at the problem IJM was trying to solve and thus create their new ambition.

At this point, while we were doing group work, the table I was at broke out into a spiky exchange. This was the difficult part, and everyone was trying to find the right lens to understand these issues, which, of course, led to a lot of disagreement.

Finally, someone said, "Well, it's simple, isn't it? All these three things are forms of modern slavery."

Someone else shot right back, "What's modern about it? It's just slavery."

Whoosh – it was like someone had poured cold water on the room as that word spread. An awkward, uncomfortable silence followed. Bodies hunched in on themselves; people crossed their arms and made themselves smaller. I could see a few people squirming in their seats. The discussion had died; no one would make eye contact. "Slavery" was a charged word in the United States, given the country's history.

The moment was rescued by an African American man, who spoke into the silence. "I think we've just confirmed we're an anti-slavery organization," he said. "And everyone is really uncomfortable right now because you don't want to offend people who look like me."

Bless him because it immediately broke the tension. "That's exactly what's happening," said his friend. "Could you help us out please?"

What IJM simplified and redefined that day, through the dialogue and work that followed, is that slavery still very much existed. Slavery in the United States was visible, outdoors, and used to be people of African origin. Today, a slave is much more likely to be a woman. She is likely to be Hispanic or Asian in origin. And you are not likely to see her because she is kept inside a factory or a sweatshop or an industrial brothel. It is a global issue.

It was a thorny, uncomfortable truth to communicate to the public. No one in that room initially felt comfortable considering it. But once they did, they realized that if they were not prepared to communicate this problem, then who would? Their new ambition became "Join us in the fight to end slavery."

Led by Tina, IJM applied the new ambition with a particular focus on the mass market and monthly giving at the time to incredible results: a rise of over 300% in three years, which is both monumental and swift.

I cannot tell you the number of nonprofits that believe they cannot find a new ambition. I have heard every excuse. *Our work is too vast. It is too varied. It is too vague.* Those organizations that can be convinced into creating a new ambition then go about it all wrong. They look for the easy, surface-level answer, the problem that is dead in the water, that is not compelling or ambitious or powerful. What IJM realized that day is that not just any ambition will do. You have to find the *right* new ambition – and it is often a truth that makes people uncomfortable. If you really think about it, that's the point. Uncomfortable people take action; comfortable people do nothing.

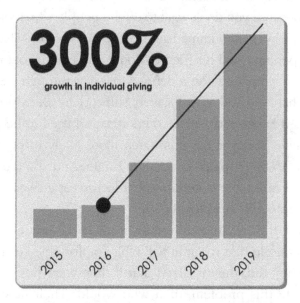

300%
growth in individual giving

2015 2016 2017 2018 2019

Figure 4.1 International Justice Mission growth chart.
Source: Revolutionise International Limited 2024.

In this chapter, I'm going to talk you through what it takes to find the right new ambition. Once you do, you can unlock the power of the impossible.

Pragmatism to Idealism

The best method I have found for discovering a new ambition that can galvanize your organization is a journey from pragmatism to idealism.

Pragmatism is when an organization is pragmatic about the reality of what they are facing. This means they need to be willing to name the problem, state it publicly, and admit that the organization has not been able to solve it as yet.

Now, more often than not, the problem is an uncomfortable truth, exactly as it was in the case of IJM. It is a truth that will demand a certain degree of organizational vulnerability. But the Great Fundraising Organizations can look this truth in the eye and work on articulating it so that the public can recognize it as well. It wasn't easy for IJM to bluntly state that slavery was at the core of their projects. It certainly was not the problem they believed they were tackling when they joined the seminar that day. But through careful and clear conversation, they found the emotional core that united their organization's projects – and then they took the courageous step of naming the problem, publicly.

So step one is you have to be pragmatic about the problem you are currently facing and you have to be able to name that problem, even if it is uncomfortable.

Step two is you have to be idealistic about tackling it.

When we received the academic research about 15 years ago and realized that all Great Fundraising Organizations had new ambitions that helped trigger their fundraising surges, the first thing we did was examine some of the most successful new ambitions in the United Kingdom. We have since repeated this exercise around the world, but here is a sample of three organizations from that original casework.

1. The National Society for the Prevention of Cruelty to Children: "Cruelty to children must stop. FULL STOP."

2. Cancer Research United Kingdom: "Together we will beat cancer."

3. Save the Children, United Kingdom: "No child born to die."

What is the first thing that jumps out at you about these new ambitions? For me, it is that they are impossible. It is impossible to stop child cruelty entirely. We cannot always beat cancer; we don't have a universal cure as yet. And there will always be children dying around the world; no single organization can prevent that, not unless they have had centuries to work on it, several mass breakthroughs in science, and several political and social circumstances aligned in their favor.

In movies about research, scientists are consistently having eureka moments. They jump out of bed because an answer came to them in a dream. They run off mid-conversation because a sentence has sparked an idea that solves the secrets of the universe. They sprint through offices, yards, houses, and parks, waving pieces of paper in the air and shouting, "I've got it! I've got it!"

Reality, I have found, is not so obliging. The life of a scientist is just sitting in front of the data, grimly trawling through it day after day and trying not to lose your mind. If you have a eureka moment, it is usually once in a decade – and even then, you are lucky.

But this was our eureka moment, and it felt like it. Every single one of the Great Fundraising Organizations' new ambitions was incredible. It was the exact opposite of what we thought we had to be: credible. The Great Fundraising Organizations were not relying on logic or evidence or methods to win donors. Instead, they wrote down the most audacious goal they could think of, and then they smacked it onto a purpose and new ambition.

All this while, we thought the driver to fundraising growth was trustworthiness. If the organization could prove to their donors they were a responsible organization that could achieve what they set out to do, then donors would give them money. But that turned out to be false. The driver wasn't logic. It was *belief*. The donor needed to believe in the problem the organization was trying to solve. If you could earn that belief, you created fundraising growth.

Take a look at those three new ambitions again. NSPCC's new ambition does not tell the donor what the organization does. Do they provide children's homes? Breakfasts at schools? Education? No clue. Cancer Research United Kingdom doesn't even have "research" in their new ambition; it is just an idealistic promise. "No child born to die" gives you no clue as to what Save the Children is about – the projects they run, the methodology they employ, nothing.

These ambitions are all idealistic visions of a future that, when viewed through a logical lens, seem impossible.

These examples deal with distant time horizons with futures that are undefined. But new ambitions can also be idealistic about a short-term future and can revolve around a focused goal.

My favorite example of this is the Cystic Fibrosis Trust in the United Kingdom. They were looking to fundraise for the fiftieth anniversary of their organization, so they were brainstorming a new ambition that would work. During the brainstorming session, one of their service users spoke up.

"I'm not comfortable celebrating the fiftieth anniversary of the organization," she said, "because I will never celebrate my fiftieth birthday."

Talk about an uncomfortable truth. It was the end of the session. How can you carry on talking about how great an organization is when it has outlived its service users? Their new ambition became a single, focused line: "We won't celebrate being fifty until everyone can."

It was a powerful, unique, and focused new ambition. It was both pragmatic about the world they lived in at the time of their fiftieth birthday and idealistic about the world they wanted to live in when they finally celebrated that birthday. (A notable postscript: This story is from some time ago. Since then, new medications have become available that mean the woman featured now has a very good chance of living into her fifties and beyond. How wonderful!)

To create a new ambition that works, you need to travel down this same journey of being pragmatic in the present but idealistic about the future. You have to be anchored in and logical about the reality you are tackling, but you must also be utterly idealistic about changing that reality.

This is what distinguishes Great Fundraising Organizations. They are credible charities with incredible ambitions.

Why, What, How

Let's dig a little deeper into this idea of idealism and how it connects to our communications hierarchy. Any sales or fundraising transaction has two stages to it: (1) inspire the desire to purchase or give and (2) overcome the objections.

In fundraising terms, we can translate this into three stages:

1. Why you should make a donation

2. What we will spend the donation on

3. How we will prove to you that we will spend it well

Theory of change communications are usually focused on the "what" and "how." This is because they apply to grant-giving bodies that plan to give out the money anyway, so what a charity needs to do to get the money is explain their "what" and "how" to distinguish themselves from their competitors.

In fundraising, however, the "what" and the "how" are only useful in overcoming the donor's objections. Once the donor has decided to give, the "what" shows the donor how the organization can provide value for money, and the "how" proves that the organization is a low-risk investment.

But the decision to give itself is always driven by the "why." It is what the donor needs in order to believe in your objective and want to be a part of it. This is why your fundraising communications must speak about the problem rather than just the success of your organization.

Exactly as the three new ambitions mentioned earlier proved, a good new ambition is not *what* you do. It is *why*. It is an audacious goal based on an uncomfortable reality, and it cannot appeal to logic or the nitty-gritty: it must inspire belief.

Differentiate Your Organization

A good new ambition also explains how your organization is different from the rest. It does this through four levers.

Problem

This is a unique problem your organization is poised to solve that aligns with your purpose. It must be an external problem, not an internal one (as we discussed in Chapter 3). Problems are often uncomfortable truths and involve organizational vulnerability, but it is important that charities name the problem clearly and not shy away from it.

Proposed Solution

This is your organization's answer to the problem that the donor is positioned to help you solve. Bear in mind that a proposed solution is not a detailed solution; a new ambition never describes the "how" or "what" of an organization. A proposed solution is simply a grand, idealistic answer to the problem. Think of it as an inspiring call to action.

In "Join us in the fight to end slavery," the goal of ending slavery would be the proposed solution. Similarly, in "Together, we will beat cancer," the proposed solution is to defeat this illness (i.e. the word "beat"). In "Child abuse must stop. FULL STOP," the proposed solution would be to stop child abuse.

None of these new ambitions provide details of how these proposed solutions can be achieved. They are big-picture, idealistic answers to the problem and focus on the "why."

Personality

This is your organizational tone of voice, which conveys a sense of your charity's character and overall approach.

Passion

Think of passion as the empathetic relationship you forge with your donor. It answers the question, *What emotion can we display to activate similar emotions and inspire the donor to give?*

These are the four levers that can create a new ambition that differentiates your organization from the others. Two of these levels (problem and proposed solution) are logical, but two of these levers are emotional (personality and passion). You need the skills and courage to work in both.

Checklist for a Good Ambition

So far, we have covered the two big fundamentals of a new ambition, which are pragmatism to idealism, and differentiating your organization from your competitors. These are two powerful methodologies that can help you view your organization and the work you do through the correct lens to discover your new ambition.

Once you arrive at potential new ambitions, however, I suggest running the options through this checklist to see if your new ambition is compelling enough to inspire fundraising growth.

- Fast
- Simple

- Active

- Ambitious

- Inspiring

- Emotional

- Fundraising built-in

- Problem and proposed solution

A new ambition should be *fast*, which means it must be easily understood by a complete stranger in a few seconds. To achieve this, it must be as *simple* as possible. Our research proves that the *active* new ambitions are the most successful: these are ambitions that include a call to action or a direct request to do something. Similarly, as we have seen in this chapter so far, an *ambitious* new ambition is a must: the more audacious the goal, the more inspiring it is.

And a good new ambition must be *inspiring*; the goal is to inspire people to action, rather than educate them toward understanding. To achieve this, a new ambition must be crafted in a predominantly *emotional* space; this means it must focus on the "why," rather than the "what" or "how."

Lastly, a powerful new ambition always has *fundraising built in*, which means it focuses on the pragmatic *problem* and the idealistic *proposed solution*.

Here is what a new ambition is not: it is not a passive description designed to logically reassure people that your organization is good at what you do. This does not work. Fundraising communications always focus on the problem, on the "why." Let the rest of the organization focus on the solution.

Illustration: Stichting het Gehandicapte Kind, the Netherlands

In wealthy countries, raising money for disability charities can be difficult because the assumption is that the health services provide everything a disabled person might need. On one level, this assumption is correct: in countries like the Netherlands, New Zealand, and Germany, a disabled person's medical needs are met fairly well by the state. But this is only one's medical needs. For a truly fulfilling life, there is a lot more that one requires.

Stichting het Gehandicapte Kind (SGK, previously named NSGK), the Dutch Society for Disabled Children, is an organization in the Netherlands focused on children with disabilities. Along with our longstanding Dutch partners, Nassau Fundraising, we ran a seminar in Holland with them, and what I loved about it was they had all the major stakeholders in the room: the fundraising department, the direct service providers, and parents of disabled children. It meant that if we reached alignment in that room, we reached alignment across the organization.

Their conflict was about how to fundraise in a society that believed disabled needs were already met by the state. We began with the usual *What problem are you trying to solve now?* They came up with hundreds of answers, which we were able to reduce to a (relative) handful, such as identity, friends, exploring, developing, for life, happiness, connecting, exercise, learning, growing, fun, being seen, opportunity, adopting, for the future, belonging, self-esteem.

We now had 20 or so problems that they were trying to solve. It led to an immediate argument. We advised that they needed to focus on only one problem, but they couldn't agree on which one it should be. Others argued that they had to solve them all, otherwise they were not providing a fulfilling life for disabled children.

This is the point at which I asked them to step away from logic. There was no point in trying to further reduce these 20 problems; they had already come down from a hundred. What they needed to do was put those problems on hold and move into an emotional space.

To do that, we shifted to storytelling. Everyone in that room had a story. Either they were a disabled adult who had lived their childhood with a disability, they were a parent of a child with a disability, or they had spent decades working with disabled children. But the story that eventually unlocked the organization's block came from their CEO, Henk-Willem Laan.

Henk-Willem's son, Joas, has a rare genetic condition that put him in and out of hospital and meant a long battle for good healthcare. It also meant that Henk-Willem took a very long time to be able to play with his son, but slowly, over years, they developed a form of play that worked.

One day, Henk-Willem was taking Joas to school on the tram. The other children were ignoring Joas. Henk-Willem's heart clenched. If there is one thing you never want to see as a parent, it is your child being ostracized. This was discrimination, and he was ready to fight to protect his child and kick up any fuss he had to.

What he discovered, however, is that it was not discrimination at all. It was a misunderstanding.

Henk-Willem and Joas played peekaboo at home. Henk-Willem would lift the blanket to hide his face and then drop it with a happy "peekaboo," which always made his son laugh. When Joas went to school, he tried to play the same game with the other children. He

(continued)

(continued)

lifted the blanket to hide his face, waiting for them to say "peekaboo" so he could drop it.

But the children had never played peekaboo before. They thought that Joas was hiding from them. They assumed he wanted to be left alone.

All it took to include Joas in the games again was teaching a class full of Dutch children peekaboo. Fifteen minutes later, Joas had friends to play with at school.

Henk-Willem first told this story to a small group of us over breakfast. We were awed. Later, Henk-Willem repeated it to the seminar delegates, and his leadership by example unlocked the entire process and the emotional confidence of everyone in the room to tell their truths as well.

It was such a powerful story. Everyone in that seminar room had felt the hurt of not having someone to play with. Parents of children with disabilities had felt Henk-Willem's pain. It fired up the room. Ideas were flying everywhere; people were so inspired, they were mixing Dutch and English. Someone said, "The most serious activity you can participate in is play." The social workers present took that further. They said, "If the children have people to play with, then given enough time, we will solve all the other problems."

Their hypothetical new ambition became "No disabled child should have to play alone." They then iterated on that new ambition to finalize "No disabled child without friends" because it allowed them to speak to a wider audience.

It was a differentiated new ambition, one that was highly emotional and that highlighted a unique problem. It struck a chord with the public. Over five to six years, on the back of the revenue they generated, they became a Great Fundraising Organization in the Netherlands.

As they were growing in revenue and popularity, SGK continued their search for simplicity. In preparation for a second fundraising surge, they changed their name from NSGK to Stichting het Gehandicapte Kind (Society for Disabled Children), which is simpler. Then they sat down and looked for a fresh new ambition to trigger a new Red Dot.

This time, the organization itself was different. It was bigger, more grownup, with more possibility and reach. After careful discussion, they realized that the problem they were tackling was still fundamentally the same: no disabled child should play alone. But for this second fundraising surge, they looked at the wider implications of this problem.

We all have empathy for a child without friends. But the consequences of playing alone extend far beyond that moment. A childhood spent alone can mean a lifetime of loneliness. It can mean a broken sense of self and an array of trauma. It alters the course of one's adulthood.

SGK changed their ambition from "No child should have to play alone" to "No child should face a lifetime of loneliness." Same problem. Much bigger impact.

When you make a nuanced shift like this between ambitions, the external communications do not change much. But the impact within the organization is astronomical. By redefining their new ambition, SGK managed to realign an expanded organization with greater capacity, streamline it behind a bigger ambition, and create a whole new level of fundraising growth.

Nor was this fresh ambition just a strapline. They had case studies and examples of how loneliness had permanently impacted a child's life.

(continued)

(continued)

SGK is now growing rapidly. They operate in a crowded market and had to carve out their own niche with rigorous testing and learning over a couple of years, before growth really started to accelerate. Given their market conditions, I consider SGK's performance to be one of the strongest I have witnessed anywhere, with growth of 76%. Last week, Henk-Willem emailed me to say he was now certain this is the beginning of a decade of unprecedented growth for the cause he and his teams are so committed to.

Stichting het Gehandicapte Kind

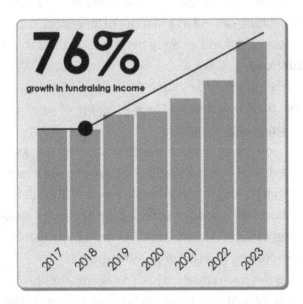

Figure 4.2 Stichting het Gehandicapte Kind growth chart.
Source: Revolutionise International Limited 2024.

Key Takeaways

If you think your organization's work is too varied to create a single new ambition, think again. You need a new ambition to begin the process of triggering the Red Dot. Every charity I have worked with has been able to find one that pushes them closer to their purpose, aligns their two businesses, and inspires all stakeholders to create meaningful change.

But to do this, you have to find the right new ambition. There are two fundamentals to creating a good new ambition. First, you have to journey from pragmatism about the present toward idealism about the future. Second, you have to articulate what differentiates your organization from others.

The number one mistake charities make is that they believe a new ambition has to be proof of credibility, so that it can inspire trust. But in actuality, it is the opposite. A new ambition must inspire belief, and belief and trust are not the same thing. Belief is our ability to imagine, hold, and participate in constructs that are abstract, including those that don't exist. Money, countries, limited liability organizations: these are not tangible things, simply a paradigm of rules. Yet our belief in them and our willingness to participate in them makes the world go round.

Believing in our ability to do impossible things is unique to human beings; it is a genetic trait we developed thousands of years ago. It is that belief that makes a donor click on your website or ring up your organization or sign the donation sheet outside a mall. Your job is to give them something to believe in.

Fundraising sells the problem; the rest of the organization sells the solution.

Chapter 5

Investment and Ambition

Let me tell you a story of an organization that got it wrong.

Out of politeness, we won't name names. It was a large organization that was fairly stable, but they were struggling with a financial deficit in the year and so called us in to see what they were doing wrong. We gave them a masterclass on everything we are covering in this book. I talked to them about the two businesses, the donor's needs, and the three blocks of the Trifecta: the new ambition, culture, and finance. Finance was a big one; it was, after all, why everyone was here.

"For transformational income," I told them, "you need transformational ambition. You need to start with a long-term problem – that is your new ambition – and based on it, you need to set your financial aspiration. Once you do that, it is just math. You calculate backward to see what financial targets you need for each year to meet your financial aspiration, and according to that, you find out the level of investment you require."

So far so good, right? My first clue everything wasn't going well was when a member of the senior leadership team approached me after a session. "Thanks for all that," he said. "We don't really care about the donor. We just want them to shut up and give us the money."

Well, what a lovely chap, I thought. *I hope I don't have to see him too often.*

The seminar series ended and the organization went to work, ostensibly to create their new ambition and get the other two blocks of the Trifecta together. But instead, they got back in touch. *We have reviewed the materials*, they said, *and we don't need all this. Nor do we have the time to implement it. We have a deficit for next year and we just need to plug it. Fix that. That's all we need.*

Now, it doesn't work like this. There are some people who will pick up this book and think, *Yippee, in two months, we'll be rich*. But the whole point of this book is that short-term thinking does not work – not if you want a powerful surge in revenue and sustainable growth. Think back to the study by Giles Pegram that we covered in Chapter 1. You have to take the long-term view for this to work, and you must implement all three blocks of the Trifecta to trigger a Red Dot. Above all, you really do have to care about the donor.

I explained this to them, while also explaining that "plugging a yearly deficit" was not the brief they gave us when they called us in. If it had been, I would not have come. They replied with swearing. *We hired you for a f****** job, so do the job. Fix our deficit.*

I pointed out that they had considerable reserves they could use to cover that deficit *and* that could also be used for investment to begin the fundraising growth cycle I had described. Of course, they would have to pick a long-term goal to work toward and align their culture toward that goal, as well as develop more respect for the fundraising team, but they could do it.

They replied with more swearing. According to them, they were not an organization that liquidated their reserves; this was not how they did things. If they were going to liquidate their reserves, they would not have hired me. Why wouldn't I just do my f****** job and fix the f****** deficit?

At this point, I knew there was no winning. There are not many organizations I walk away from, but there was no point in persevering. I wished them well – they replied with more swearing – and then watched as slowly, across the space of a year, every single one of their fundraising team resigned. I don't blame them. How are you supposed to succeed when the rest of the organization has no respect for you and sees you as a cash cow expected to work miracles? The charity still survives, but it is considerably smaller – although I don't doubt they have lovely, lush reserves.

Compare this with St. Catherine's Hospice. The chair of trustees was Terry O'Leary, who joined the organization under unusual circumstances. Terry used to be managing director of a global bank before retiring in 2013. That year, his wife got diagnosed with lung cancer, so he spent the first year of his retirement caring for her. It soon became apparent the cancer was terminal, at which point they began getting her care from St Catherine's Hospice, which they knew of through reputation and their friends. Terry was incredibly touched by how the organization cared for his wife. When she died, he joined as their trustee.

I held our seminar series with St. Catherine's Hospice at our Loch Ness Center, which is a stunning location to have a conversation. All the big stakeholders from St. Catherine's Hospice were in attendance, so we had the CEO, the director of fundraising, several members of the board and senior leadership, and, of course, Terry. Every time we took a break, Terry went for a walk to process what we had just discussed, a practice I had a lot of sympathy for because I do the same. On the day we covered the second block of the Trifecta, finance and investment, Terry went on a longer walk than usual. I had told St. Catherine's Hospice the same thing I told the organization that wanted me to fix their deficit: about thinking long-term, finding a financial aspiration, and calculating backward.

"The mistake charities make," I said, "is they believe they are asking for money. They are not. What they are doing is *earning* money."

When Terry came back from his walk, he was absolutely beaming. What on earth had happened on that walk?

Investment and Ambition

"I realized something, that is all," Terry said. "I realized why I am here."

If you are looking for a book that fixes your organization's annual deficit or that acts as a miracle growth pill, then this is not the book for you. But if you are like Terry, and you are eager to help an organization you believe in unlock the next level of growth, then you are in the right place. When Terry joined St. Catherine's Hospice as someone who had spent his career in the private sector, he didn't know what value he could bring to a charity. Our research on finance showed him the role he was meant to play. If there is one thing a managing director in the private sector knows, it is how to earn money.

So how do you earn money? How do you trigger the next block of the Trifecta, which is finance and investment? You remember the golden rule:

Transformational income depends on transformational ambition.

Deciding Your Financial Aspiration

There is a reason we start with the new ambition as the first block of the Trifecta: it sets the tone and focus for the next two blocks, investment and culture.

Organizations that stagnate set their budget and financial goals on an annual basis. They look at their spreadsheets, ask *How much money did we raise last year?* and then add 5% to that number to get their financial goal for the coming year.

Great Fundraising Organizations, on the other hand, begin by setting their new ambition. The new ambition gives them a goal to work toward, a long-term problem they want to solve. Once they know that goal, they can set a financial aspiration. This is the revenue they believe they must earn to eradicate that long-term problem and achieve the new ambition. After you set your financial aspiration, then it is just math: you calculate backward to see how much revenue you need to generate per year to meet your financial aspiration and then how much investment you need to generate that annual revenue.

Hang on, you say. *You told us that a new ambition has to be idealistic – impossible even. How are we meant to set a financial target based on an idealistic, impossible goal?*

Excellent question. You do it by putting all the stakeholders in the room and talking it through.

When Scotland's Charity Air Ambulance came to us, they were looking for a purpose and fundraising ambition "for the next 10 years" following an outstanding market entry in the previous decade. Now they were looking to enhance and expand their services to quickly reach the most remote areas in Scotland. Here, the need was not only to get the person to a hospital; it was far more urgent to get medical practitioners to the injured person so they could administer first aid at the scene. We discussed it and formulated a new ambition: "Help must always get there in time." This was based on the statement of the problem "Nobody should suffer or die because help cannot get to them in time."

You will notice that, as usual, the ambition was grand, idealistic, and almost impossible (help cannot always get there in time). In other words, it was perfect. They had their goal; now they needed a financial aspiration to match it. How much money did they think they would need to ensure help always got there in time?

I was in the room when they did this exercise; they brought together all the stakeholders – senior leadership, the board (including representation from the Scottish Ambulance Service), and the full charity team. It immediately became apparent that the services department was the most conservative about the amount they believed they could fundraise. The fundraising team – no surprises there – was the most ambitious and confident. This was a safe space;

everyone was respectful and honest with each other and had a fantastic relationship, so the discrepancy didn't seem problematic, just funny. All the members of the board who had worked in the private sector almost immediately took the side of the fundraising team, and so the bar was set to ambitious.

Then they asked me, *Who are the comparable organizations in Scotland that we can use to figure out scale?* I named the Children's Hospices Across Scotland, along with their general revenue. Instantly, the fundraising team got competitive. (Again, *excellent* instincts in a fundraising team.)

Once they had that, they asked me about the best global nonprofits I could think of in the fundraising space so they could use it as a benchmark. I thought for a bit and then told them about Børns Vilkår, the Danish organization that focused on children's rights, among others. I also observed that the best fundraising organizations I had studied managed to achieve a revenue of about £12 for every man, woman, and child in their country's population. In Scotland, this would equate to creating a total revenue of more than £60 million per year.

Sixty million. There was a hush in the room as everyone contemplated the number. This was a big figure, far larger than they had imagined. Once it had sunk in, the conversation changed. It became *How many years will we need to reach that?* This went around for a while before they settled on their interim target for the next 10 years, which was truly aspirational and scales of magnitude more than they had achieved with their early successes. David Craig, the CEO, reflected for some time and then backed the huge ambition openly, stating that it was necessary to fulfill the charity's purpose. The fundraisers were off the leash.

Using that figure, they worked backward to create a financial plan – i.e. the amount of investment they would need to generate that revenue, growing every year for the next 5–10 years.

The process will look similar in your organization. In my experience, there are usually three stakeholders in a room when deciding a nonprofit's financial aspiration: the fundraisers, the administrators, and the service users. The service users tend to stay out of the conversation because it is not their expertise. The administrators are conservative about the financial aspiration because they are used to dealing with budgetary deficits and annual financial needs. The fundraisers just get competitive; they want to beat every other charity when it comes to generating fundraising revenue. Together, based on the nonprofit's new ambition, these stakeholders decide a financial aspiration and then create a financial plan that can make that aspiration a reality.

Organizations that stagnate base their investment plans on budgetary needs. Great Fundraising Organizations base it on financial aspirations.

The Power of Long-Term Thinking

To crack the second block of the Trifecta, a charity has to shift from a governance mindset to a growth mindset. We've covered this mindset shift in detail in Chapter 2, but I mention it here because it is crucial to implementing this Trifecta block. Without a growth mindset, an organization is precisely like the one I walked away from: seeking to fill short-term budgetary gaps with short-term solutions. A growth mindset, on the other hand, keeps a charity's perspective firmly on the long-term – and it judges the investment it makes based on that long-term.

Why is long-term thinking so vital when it comes to finances? If we step back and look at the big picture of organizations progressing toward fulfilling their purpose, then it is my conclusion – based on a very large dataset – that almost everyone overestimates what can be achieved in 1 year in terms of organizational progress and financial growth. However, they grossly underestimate what can be achieved in 10 years.

The difference between what is possible in 1 year versus what is possible in 10 is often in multiples, and it is difficult for the human mind to comprehend the difference. Why is the gap so large? The reason is compound growth, which is a hundred little things improving by 1% over a sustained period of time, creating an avalanche of progress.

Below is a chart that shows how a 1% improvement over time compounds in terms of gains and how a 1% loss compounds in terms of decline. What begins as a negligible gap grows gradually over time into a startling difference.

Compound growth can be difficult to imagine because we often don't mentally adjust for how success changes the baseline. Every year, an organization starts from a higher base due to the success

Compound growth (or decline) based on marginal developments

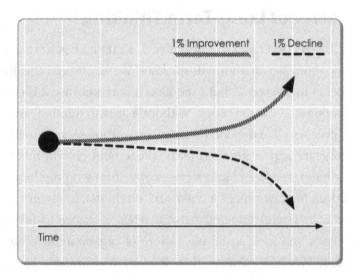

Figure 5.1 Compound growth (or decline) based on marginal developments.

Source: Revolutionise International Limited 2024.

Great Fundraising Organizations

of the previous year, which means the gain in the current year is bigger – even if the percent increase stays exactly the same – simply because the starting point is higher.

Let's take another look at the client growth charts that we featured in the Introduction.

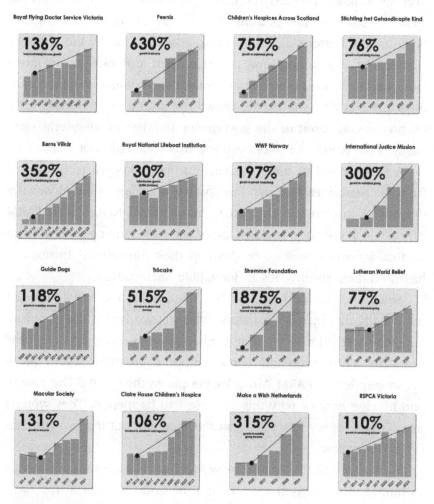

Figure 5.2 Growth charts for a selection of Great Fundraising Organizations.

Source: Revolutionise International Limited 2024.

You can clearly see how the growth rate is not only maintained but in fact accelerates over the period of the time, sometimes dramatically and sometimes just relentlessly. It is the compound effect, which is why the long-term view is so vital.

Being able to predict not only growth but compound growth over the long-term means you can make much more reliable investment decisions in the present. It is a way of future-proofing the organization. Better still, if you can predict and model the different elements of your fundraising portfolio, then it allows you to move money around to maximize opportunities according to market conditions. (This is why we say the growth mindset is so important for a charity, as compared to the governance mindset. A long-term view changes the game and offers you rewards you could not imagine.)

A close friend of mine, Richard Turner, is known to the world for some reason as "Haggis." Twenty-five years ago, Richard was the director of fundraising for a small international NGO called FARM Africa, which conducts research into sustainable farming in East Africa so that farmers can start or develop their agricultural businesses based on their insights. It's an incredible organization.

Since then, Richard has left the organization and moved on, but he recently met up with someone who still worked at the nonprofit and who told him of a strange phenomenon. Over the past few years, the organization had seen a compound growth in legacy gifts – i.e. money left to FARM Africa by people in their wills. The charity had no clue how or why this increase had happened. They weren't investing in legacy fundraising at the moment, but the growth continued regardless.

Richard found the story to be wonderful because it wasn't strange to him at all. Twenty-five years ago, he and the CEO at the time, Christie Peacock, worked with the board to invest in legacy fundraising. That single campaign was a success and brought on a whole new influx of pledgers to FARM Africa.

Twenty-five years later, those donors – who had maintained a steady relationship with FARM Africa over the decades – were passing on, and their wills were coming into effect. Hence the influx of legacy income for the organization, which the present team were baffled by.

That is the power of long-term thinking. A single campaign 25 years ago created a surge of growth that was still growing decades later. An investment of a few thousand pounds created a total income, over time, of millions.

Understanding Investment

There is a particular kind of person in every charity who thinks they know everything about fundraising without knowing anything at all. We like to call them ALOOFs: Amateurs with a Lot of Opinions on Fundraising. In the masterclasses I do, at least one ALOOF will ask me, *Why do we need investment for fundraising? Surely it is the job of fundraising to bring in the money, not require it.*

It is indeed the job of fundraising to bring in the money, but they cannot do that without investment. Fundraising is not a golden goose; there is no magic involved. To generate revenue, fundraising has only two avenues:

1. Get an existing donor to give more money to the organization

2. Convert a new person into becoming a donor

The first point is by far the best way to increase fundraising revenue in an organization, but to achieve this at any effective level, fundraising first must do the second point. And to convert a new person into becoming a donor, you need investment.

Look at the imperfect but very useful donor pyramid below, which shows the different types of fundraising avenues created across the lifetime of a donor. Which one do you think is the hardest to achieve?

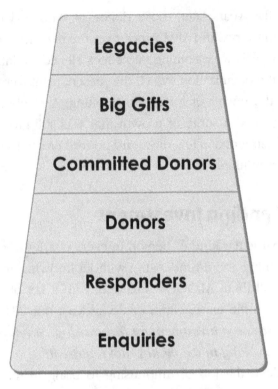

Figure 5.3 Donor pyramid.
Source: Reprinted with permission from Ken Burnett, Relationship Fundraising, 2002/2024.

If you ask an ALOOF, they will tell you it is the lifetime legacy donation, which is when a donor bequeaths a nonprofit a sum of money in their will. In actuality, this is the easiest to achieve. By this point, a donor has stuck with the organization through all the levels of the pyramid, shown clear loyalty to the charity, and is more than willing to give the nonprofit a lasting gift that can help them better serve their service users. The toughest tier, as you have probably guessed, is the first tier: getting a donor to make the first donation. This is why you need investment: to get the right materials that differentiate you from your competition and to cast a wide enough net, as effectively as possible, to convert leads into donors.

From then on, the fundraising team can focus on keeping the donor and progressing them through the levels of the pyramid. This does not need as much investment as the first push of securing a donor, but it does require some money. To keep a donor, you must meet your donors' needs, and that often means letters, updates, thank you notes, and other tokens. You have to make them feel appreciated.

I knew someone once who focused his donations on organizations that worked with children. He donated a very large amount of money to a national children's charity, which took the money – they cashed the check – and never got in touch with him again. They didn't give any token of appreciation, not even a simple email to say thank you. So he said, *Screw this*, and redirected his funds to Hope House, the small, local hospice in the area where his donations made a larger difference. He is happier. So is the hospice. The only player who lost out is the national children's charity that didn't bother to say thank you.

Types of Investments

Let's break down the different areas you need to invest in to ensure fundraising growth and that you must take into account when creating your financial plan. There are two types of fundraising investment:

1. Sunk costs: This is an investment in your organization's infrastructure, such as systems, tools, communication platforms, etc. It is best to see these as costs that cannot be helped and cannot be recovered; they create the infrastructure you need to run an effective fundraising business.

2. Rolling investments: These are investments that yield returns and directly contribute to creating fundraising growth. They can be further divided into two categories: media and people. "Media" refers to all the marketing materials, communications, visuals, advertisements, videos, etc. – essentially, anything the fundraising team needs to communicate the organization's new ambition to potential leads and convert them into donors. "People" refers to the fundraising team, which are the people behind the fundraising efforts.

Sources of Investment

There are three different sources of investment for fundraising growth:

- Reserves
- Revenue
- Grants, donations, loans

Most charities will have financial reserves; it is possible to break these and redirect the funds toward investing in fundraising growth. Several of the charities we work with choose this route because it allows them the most freedom and autonomy. Having seen Giles Pegram's chart, they also know it has the most impact and benefit to the future of the organization.

The second route is to pull the investment money out of the organization's existing annual revenue budget. This can be difficult to achieve because it sometimes means freeing up money from elsewhere, which usually translates into redirecting funds away from service users. In Chapter 1, we mentioned the trolley dilemma when discussing the investment conflict. Pulling money out of the annual revenue budget to redirect it into fundraising evokes the trolley dilemma. Is it better to use the money immediately to save one service user, or is it better to invest the money in fundraising to save many more service users down the line? It is not an easy decision, especially because fundraising does not operate in the short-term and a nonprofit will not see the results of their reinvestment for a while. It remains one of the hardest decisions leadership has to make.

For those organizations that can only find a modest sum of money to invest in fundraising, one option is to invest that sum and then reinvest most (or even all) of the fundraising returns back into fundraising to drive growth faster. We've seen this done to great effect. Usually, the board, senior leadership, and the fundraising team agree in advance that reinvestment is the path they will follow, and then the organization begins pulling out fundraising profits only once fundraising has reached a certain size. It is a smart way to engineer growth if your organization does not have available cash for fundraising investment.

The third option is to seek money from third parties, such as grants, funding bodies, and banks. On the surface, this might seem like the best option – using outside money in the form of grants or loans as an investment injection to spur fundraising growth. But it is not a great avenue because it slows down fundraising so that the team cannot move quickly or build momentum. Moreover, a nonprofit tends to give up control once they accept outside money, which can hinder how effectively they can fundraise. It is the avenue with the least success.

Calculating Investment

Let's say you have set your financial aspiration and know how much revenue you plan to generate per year to achieve your new ambition. How do you calculate how much *investment* you require to create that fundraising revenue?

There is a simple formula for this: you look at your historical data, you look at similar organizations that can serve as your benchmarks, you arrive at a number, and then you keep refining that number as you move forward. Remember, as we said in Chapter 2, the Trifecta is a leadership problem: each block is a goal, an aspiration, and you have to keep iterating on the steps as you progress toward that goal. My colleague Fiona McPhee, our director in Australia and New Zealand, has spent over a decade refining benchmarking data and models. The effect on boards when they see exactly what other organizations can achieve is transformational.

Also remember that the Trifecta only works when all three blocks are implemented. It is very easy at this stage to get fired up about finance and investment, and think that you have the secret to success in your hands. But don't go rushing to the board or the senior leadership with a calculated investment amount and a watertight plan for fundraising growth. You cannot implement this plan effectively without the other two blocks of the Trifecta: the new ambition and culture. Moreover, you are likely to ruin any chance of leadership buy-in if you move immediately. Trust me, you need all three. Go through these steps one by one. Your goal is to trigger Red a Dot, yes – but it is also to keep triggering it, over and over, to become a Great Fundraising Organization. This is the bigger prize.

Illustration: Børns Vilkår, Denmark

Børns Vilkår is a Danish children's rights organization. When we met them, they were looking to rebrand. Their fundraising growth was steady, but they were suffering in the mass market segment and wanted to accelerate growth because they knew it would give them greater freedom and mobility. Their CEO, Rasmus Kjeldahl, is one of the best, most focused people I've ever had the pleasure of meeting. He is just excellent at anything he puts his mind to. Luckily for Børns Vilkår, he put his mind to transforming the organization and standing up for children.

This was in the early days for us. We had just studied the academic dataset, so we knew the insights we wanted to share with people, and we knew how transformative those insights could be, but we were not sure about the best way in which to tell them. Our seminar series was focused on convincing clients about the worth of what we had found and less on the practical. Rasmus changed all that.

Midway through our seminar series, Rasmus disappeared to hold a conference call. When he came back, he told me that he had just got off the phone with the organization that was doing their rebranding; he had asked them to pause so that Børns Vilkår could complete our seminars and implement our insights in their rebranding. A day later, he came to me again. "I'm convinced this works, Alan," he said. "I don't need more evidence. What I need is a to-do list. Give me a list of how to implement this and I will make it happen."

So I made a list. I wiped down the whiteboard and wrote it out, step by step. That moment transformed Børns Vilkår, but it also transformed our organization; the seminar series has never been the same since.

Once he had the list, Rasmus worked through it with laser focus. First, he took our insights from the seminar series and shared them with the wider organization. He convinced the board and senior leadership to back him up on the changes he wanted to make.

Then he gathered the charity's major stakeholders and set out to create their new ambition. They knew their purpose: to protect the rights of minors. But what was their goal for the next 10 years? What problem were they looking to solve? They settled on a powerful new ambition, which, in Danish, was "Stop Svigt." In English, it translates into "Stop the culpable neglect of children." It sounds horribly unwieldy in English, but it has an enormous impact in Danish.

(continued)

(continued)

The next thing I knew, I was in Denmark for a work meeting when I got a call from Rasmus. "Free for a coffee?" he asked. I met him at the nearest coffee shop during my break, we sat down, and he launched straight into it. "How do I recruit the best fundraisers?" he said.

I knew Rasmus; if he wanted the very best, he would get them. Months later, Lisbet Christoffersen had joined Børns Vilkår as director of fundraising, and after a few years of investment and success, Allan Laursen joined as head of individual giving. They were absolutely instrumental in taking that new ambition and driving the investment and financial plan that put Børns Vilkår's fundraising at the heart of driving their mission forward so much. Over the next few years, Lisbet and Allan's expertise guided the organization through uncharted waters and changed the game for them.

But Rasmus was not done. There was still one more thing on our to-do list: culture. He instituted an organization-wide training program that taught his staff how to recognize the needs of the donors and support the fundraising team in the materials they needed to succeed.

Seven years later, Børns Vilkår has gone from being a modest, niche player in the mass marketing segment to dominating market share. They have the most donors, with the total number of people giving having increased by 626%. They never would have seen those results if they had given up in year one, two, or even five.

Børns Vilkår exemplifies what it means to invest in multiple segments to ensure your organization achieves transformational growth. And it really has been transformational. Their services reach many, many more children and families than they did seven years ago.

Great Fundraising Organizations

Børns Vilkår

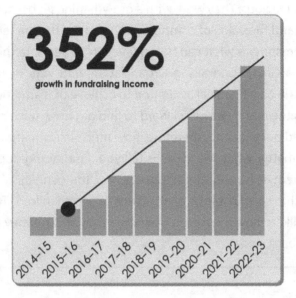

Figure 5.4 Børns Vilkår growth chart.
Source: Revolutionise International Limited 2024.

Key Takeaways

Transformational income depends on transformational ambition. This is why, to implement the second block of the Trifecta, you have to link your finances to your new ambition. You cannot think short-term, you cannot focus on only plugging a deficit, and you cannot come up with a number that is unattached to a new ambition because it will not galvanize, align, and motivate your organization – and you need those things to achieve your new financial goal.

(continued)

(continued)

Great Fundraising Organizations choose a financial aspiration that is audacious. They work with a growth mindset because they understand the value of compounding and the human tendency to underestimate what can be achieved in 10 years. To think and act like a Great Fundraising Organization, find your new ambition, settle on a financial aspiration to achieve that ambition, and then do the math: work backward to find out how much revenue you need per year and, therefore, how much investment.

No matter what the ALOOFs tell you, fundraising does need investment. It is not a golden goose. But the benefits of investing in this second block of the Trifecta are manifold. Think of Børns Vilkår: they invested in their organization, and they haven't looked back since.

Chapter 6

Culture and Ambition

Lutheran World Relief (LWR) is a midsized international nonprofit with headquarters in Baltimore, United States, but with active staff all over the world. They are a good fundraising organization; they have always managed moderate but steady growth. In 2018, however, their fundraising growth dipped. No one could pinpoint exactly why.

I wouldn't go as far as to say this created organizational panic, but it led to serious introspection within the charity. The CEO gave a clear directive to return to a strategy of rapid growth. Someone had looked at the data and suggested that the dip was due to market saturation among the Lutheran population. LWR's best chance of creating more revenue was to go secular so that they could attract a wider audience.

Instead of doing this, the two senior-most people in their fundraising team, Dave Fuerst and Eddie Byrd, attended our Loch Ness masterclass. What we discovered was that LWR struggled to articulate their new ambition or their point of differentiation from other nonprofits and that the debates within their organization were bogging them down. Dave and Eddie showed us the marketing analysis, including the suggestion to go secular, and we shook our heads. If LWR did this, they would be in a worse position than before; they would lose their point of differentiation and become exactly like any other NGO. I remember asking them, "How many people are there in the United States who identify as Lutheran?"

The answer was an estimate of 10 million people.

"Hang on," I said. "That is a huge number. It is twice as big as the population of my country. How many of them are your donors?"

A few tens of thousands.

"Right," I said. "How about we get a million out of those 10 million Lutherans, and then we'll worry about market saturation?"

Eddie and David laughed, we set aside the marketing opinion, and some weeks later, LWR flew us to Baltimore to help them create a new ambition.

This Baltimore seminar series was packed. There were about a hundred people from all over the organization, including representatives from every department: development, research, policy, fundraising, marketing, leadership – you name it. During the seminar series, LWR realized the problem they were trying to solve was that you couldn't help someone if you could not reach them.

So their new ambition became "Reach everyone in need."

Now, on the surface, this new ambition looked perfect. But there were problems with the language. This could have been the new ambition of any international NGO. It was not distinctive. What's more, this was not the language of their donors, which was the language of the Lutheran Church. In this instance, differentiation could only be found in their audience's values – in other words, personality and passion.

So, if we wanted the new ambition to be powerful and convincing, we had to find a way to reframe "Reach everyone in need." We needed the right language to create an emotional connection with their donors and meet their unique needs. Otherwise, it wouldn't work.

"This is great work," I told them, "but you are bloody Lutherans, so go away for an hour, come back, and say it the way Jesus would have said it."

That one line horrified my teammates; they all stared at me like, *Did Alan really say that?* But it absolutely galvanized LWR. They went from low energy, confused, and introspective to buzzing, animated, loud, and enthusiastic. When they came back, they were a new organization. The articulation of their problem had changed from the simple and bland "You cannot save someone if you cannot reach them" to "In a world of plenty, the people who have the least are the most forsaken." How brilliant is that? It could have been written by Martin Luther himself and pinned to the door of a church. From that problem, they articulated a new ambition in the Lutheran language: "Until your love reaches every neighbor."

But the incredible part is still to come. Having settled on their new ambition, LWR got to work creating their fundraising communications, putting their investment in place, and preparing the organization for a fundraising surge. Almost immediately, they saw a short-term revenue increase of about 25%. This was a massive immediate uplift, almost unthinkably big, to the point that I called up Dave to find out what had happened. It had not been long enough for the new ambition communications to reach the market, nor had LWR implemented any investment. What was going on?

The answer was culture. When LWR changed their language from development speak to the language of their donors, the organization transformed internally. Staff felt connected to their purpose again, and no one argued about next steps; everyone just moved at pace, and everything got done faster. It was this internal behavioral shift that led to the immediate income increase. And now that LWR had seen the income increase, they were even more driven because they believed in what they were creating.

In the middle of all this, the COVID-19 pandemic hit. Unlike many other organizations who backed off fundraising or became paralyzed by indecision, LWR accelerated through it. They brought

123

their relaunch forward and went at it even faster. Dave reports, "This would not have been possible if we had not been one voice. The team was galvanized behind the message."

This is the most dramatic example I've seen of how the third block in the Trifecta, culture, can transform a nonprofit's growth. By changing the language of the organization from development speak to donor-focused language, LWR aligned their team with the needs and interests of their donors. They made the donor a priority in the same way the service user always had been. This behavioral shift, this refocus, aligned the entire nonprofit in the right direction and spearheaded growth.

When the whole organization is as good at meeting the needs of the donors as it is at meeting the needs of service users, then you

Lutheran World Relief

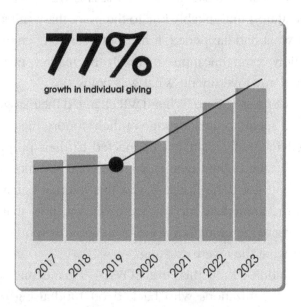

Figure 6.1 Lutheran World Relief growth chart.
Source: Revolutionise International Limited 2024.

have successfully aligned people to ambition. To do this, you must create a donor-conscious organization.

Why a Donor-Conscious Organization?

When we introduce people to the Trifecta, they are often fired up by the investment block and deeply inspired by the new ambition. Culture, however, takes a backseat. People struggle to see the value in it. In my opinion, however, cultural change is the biggest driver of revenue. If you can get your culture right, you have won half the battle.

What does it mean to "get your culture right"? Think back to Chapter 1, to the cultural conflict created by the two businesses. On the one hand, we have the services departments who speak in development speak and respect data and evidence. On the other hand, we have the fundraising team, the ambitious achievers who operate quickly in an emotional space and focus on the language of their donors. Unless you bridge that gap, your nonprofit will be marred by infighting and paralysis, which means little to no growth.

To bridge that gap, you have to get the rest of the organization (i.e. the services departments) on board with the fundraising team. It's just logical:

1. To create good revenue, the fundraising team has to attract donors. To attract those donors, they have to be better than the competition at meeting donor needs.

↓

2. To meet donor needs, the fundraising team must have the very best communications, content, materials, and insight from the rest of the organization to help them achieve this.

↓

125

3. This means that the rest of the organization must give fundraising what they need.

The problem is usually with the third point. Most nonprofits do not know what the donor needs, do not care what the donor needs, or (and this is my favorite) think the donor should need something other than what they do need. This last one is a surprisingly common attitude in the charity space. It translates into nonprofits believing that donors should be educated, guilted, or ranted at. Occasionally, charities will claim they are "too busy" and cannot (or rather will not) move quickly enough to give fundraising the right materials.

The solution to this is to create what we call "whole organization fundraising." No, it does not mean that everyone in the charity goes out and asks for money. It means that everyone in the nonprofit realizes that meeting donor needs is a strategic priority if they want to raise more money, knows what their donors' needs are, and are resourced and willing to give fundraising what they require to address donor needs better than their competitors.

The new ambition plays a big role in this because it forms an anchor for your organization. If created well, a new ambition is essentially the change in the world that your donor base is trying to achieve. Think back to Chapter 3: it is not "You have a problem. We can help solve it." It is "We have a problem. You (i.e. the donor) can help solve it." The new ambition keeps your charity's focus squarely on the donor: how the donor thinks, what they want to achieve, and why they want to achieve it.

Meeting donor needs doesn't just apply to fundraising via direct marketing to individuals. It also applies to fundraising from corporations and foundations because corporations and foundations have needs as well. Some of these needs will be clearly stated in their philanthropy policies, but some of these needs will be emotional (and perhaps more hidden) because foundations and corporations are made up of people too. Together for Short Lives understood this, which is why they rigorously implemented an analysis of donor needs when pitching to a supermarket chain worth over £10 million – and they got the partnership. Whether you are fundraising from an individual or from a corporation, the evidence is clear that it helps to be a donor-conscious organization.

What Stops Great Fundraising?

The blocks to achieving a donor-conscious organization are cultural, not structural. Here are some of the blocks we have seen:

- Over-intellectualization
- Distaste of emotion
- Obsession with image
- Fear of being criticized or looking stupid
- Power games and politics
- Fear of becoming too busy with the "extra" fundraising work, especially since the work is seen as superfluous
- Fear of commitment and effort

These are people problems. You are dealing with feelings, not logic. As Peter Drucker says, "Culture eats strategy for breakfast" when it comes to building a Great Fundraising Organization. To create whole organization fundraising, you must engineer belief and focus among your people that meeting donor needs is a good thing to do in its own right. You have to make the organization understand the importance of addressing donor needs in making more money, how that money will help them better help service users, and the crucial role they play in ensuring fundraising success. Once you do that, you will have successfully aligned people to ambition and created an organization that is aligned toward growth.

To go back to that famous line from Professor Sargeant, "The greatest block to great fundraising is internal conflict, leading to consensus-seeking compromise." In Chapter 3, we said the solution to this is internal alignment. Viewed through a cultural lens, this solution translates into "the whole organization is proud of fundraising and able to contribute to it." That's it – that's what you are reaching for. The cultural shift you are trying to make is that the nonprofit is just as proud of being a Great Fundraising Organization as it is of its work with service users. If you achieve that, you have cracked it.

Creating a Donor-Conscious Organization

There are two ways of creating a donor-conscious organization. One is an extreme method called quality management systems; it is time-consuming and expensive, but it may be the right approach if your organization is out of alignment and needs a reset. The second method, memetics, is simpler and more common and introduces donor-conscious thinking into the organization through a series of steps.

Quality Management Systems: Building Blocks for Great Fundraising

This method is a structural way in which you can rework the entire culture of your organization. It hinges around the term "quality."

The accepted and standard definition of "quality" in business is being excellent at meeting the needs of your clients. This is true across sectors. From that, we get the famous acronym QMS, which stands for quality management systems that ensure you deliver high quality consistently to your customers. It is a big industry in the private sector, with certifications (over here in the United Kingdom, we focus on ISO certifications).

We have interacted with hundreds of charities over the years, and every single one of them has QMS for their service users. These systems can be extremely detailed because they are often dealing with vulnerable people who need extra layers of protection.

In the 25 years of my career, I have only come across one nonprofit that had quality standards for its donors. One.

If you think about it, it is not surprising considering what we know about existing nonprofit thinking and the belief that meeting the needs of the service users is all that matters. To address this gap, we researched and formulated a QMS for donors, which we call the Building Blocks of Great Fundraising. Figure 6.2 shows only the top level of these blocks, and each of them can be broken down into more detail. There can be up to a hundred building blocks, depending on the organization.

Different organizations have approached QMS differently. Some of the successful organizations we have worked with have gone through the blocks from beginning to end and implemented them one by one. The most famous organization among these is the Macular Society in the United Kingdom, which realized they needed to change from a small charity to a big one because their cause had grown from small to big in the last 20 years. They worked through the building blocks with the intent to transform their organization structurally and then recruited into that new structure, thereby changing the culture from the ground up. It was quite remarkable to witness.

Others have done an audit to discover the key blocks they need to get into place to get started. One of my favorite anecdotes from this is a Danish organization that ran the audit after our masterclass.

The Building Blocks

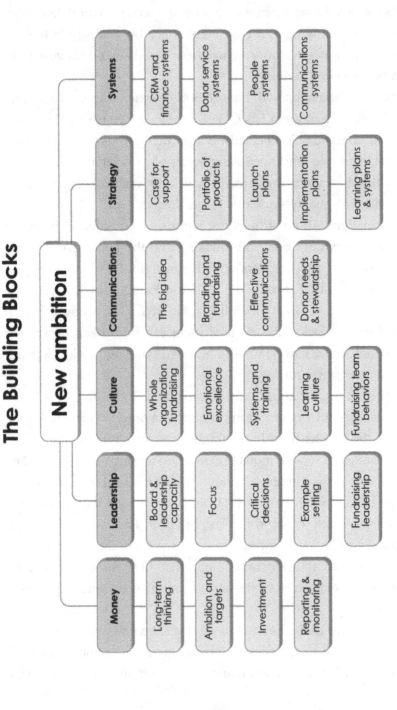

Figure 6.2 The building blocks.
Source: Revolutionise International Limited 2024.

Great Fundraising Organizations

The CEO and the fundraising director spent an hour on it. When they came back into the room, the CEO was all smiles and beaming, while the fundraising director looked very downbeat. It was so comically different, I had to ask them what was going on.

"We've done the audit," the fundraising director said, "and we have only got one of the building blocks."

"That's true," the CEO said cheerfully, "but we've got board and leadership capacity, and with that, I can get everything else."

You know what? The CEO was absolutely right.

Bear in mind that our QMS for donors is not a structural solution to solve a cultural problem. It's a structural solution to change the culture from the ground up, by transforming your whole organization. It is an extreme way of doing things, it takes time, and it takes significant investment, but by creating a QMS for fundraising and donor needs, you are structurally introducing quality service into the organization and then recruiting in line with that donor-centered culture. We are not against structural solutions, but they should be "as well as" cultural solutions, not "instead of."

Memetics

The second method to get your culture into alignment is what we call "memetics." We don't mean internet memes but the original use of the word in Richard Dawkins's book *The Selfish Gene*. In this method, you create little things (i.e. memes) that you can embed in the organization that, if they stick, replicate and change the culture. Think of it as shaping the evolution of a culture with certain markers.

This is faster than the QMS method, and we have found it to be surprisingly effective with certain clients. Here, you are not structurally introducing quality service within an organization as much as you are developing a donor-conscious nonprofit. In this method, memes are introduced into existing systems, so there is no ground-up reworking of the organization. Every meme you introduce acts as a reminder for the leadership, middle management, and the team regarding the donors' needs. It means that when anyone is making a decision, they ask themselves, *Is this in the best interests of our service users and our donors? Is it adding value to our donors as well as our service users?*

There are three things we have found that help implement the memetics method in organizations:

- Measurement
- Systems
- Training

By measurement, we mean measuring the attitude of the staff in all departments toward fundraising and donors. Organizations usually achieve this through surveys. In Børns Vilkår, they discovered that the act of measuring these attitudes automatically improved them. It was the Heisenberg effect: active observation or active measurement changes what is being observed or measured.

The second step is systems, by which we mean the big abstract systems: leadership, communications, finance, volunteers, etc. Here, we are looking at the little things we can introduce into existing systems so that stakeholders remember donor needs, especially when making decisions. We often call these memes "What would Marjorie need"? If you recall, Marjorie is the elderly donor for CBM whose loneliness and loyalty became a catalyst for CBM to change their attitude toward donors. Different organizations have different names for this influential donor. At Børns Vilkår, for example, she is called Gitte. By focusing on a Marjorie or a Gitte, the non-profit's many departments remember that donors are human and with desires.

Here are a few examples of memes you could introduce into existing systems to keep the donor top of mind:

- Ask for money in every communication so people always remember there are donors funding this.

- Ensure fundraising gets to sign off on communications from other departments to confirm they meet donor needs, as well as have a lead role in brand design.

- Make sure all staff have a powerful fundraising story and elevator pitch.

- Pin stories of donors all around the office. The reception and the back of toilet doors are the two most effective places for people to read stories. Put them up there alongside stories of service users so that both the donor and the service user are top of mind.

- Put fundraising needs on every meeting agenda, particularly board and senior management meetings. Ninety-five percent of these meetings will be about service users, which is necessary, but spend the remaining 5% checking if you are doing the best for your donors.

- Implement an HR system with a basic understanding of donor needs, and include a focus on the donor in recruitment, inductions, and appraisals.

But the biggest meme of all is introducing donor needs into decision-making criteria. Just as you have questions like *How does this focus our resources?* or *How does this benefit our service users?*, ask the question *How does this benefit our donor?* Make it a compulsory question people have to answer before a decision is finalized and authorized. This is the single most powerful meme you can inject into any organization.

The third step is training. Train the board in donor needs, then train the leadership team, then the entire organization. After that, put it in the onboarding training – or induction training, as we call it in the United Kingdom – so that you are teaching recruits to think about donor needs from the get-go. Make sure you continue the training on an ongoing basis. This way, you create an organization that excels at knowing what your donor wants and at meeting those needs.

Illustration: Salvation Army, Australia, and Guide Dogs, United Kingdom

Most organizations have an instinctive idea of what donors need. You just have to ask the right people.

The Salvation Army is one of the biggest fundraising organizations in Australia. They are so loved they have a nickname: the Salvos. You say that name in Australia, and there is instant brand recognition. The people who work for them on the ground are called the Salvation Army officers, and they have almost universal respect in the country. These are generally quite humble and soft-spoken people, but they are faith driven and astonishingly resilient. They dedicate their entire lives, on very modest salaries, to helping the downtrodden, and they often live in the projects themselves: in drug projects, with homeless people, with vulnerable populations.

We have worked with Salvos for close to 10 years now, including helping them as they went through a complicated merger of their two massive organizations, Australia East (based in Sydney) and Australia South (based in Melbourne). Both organizations had vastly different cultures before the merger, and we found that Salvos could easily get bogged down with internal conflicts, differences of opinion, and complexity.

We knew the donors for Salvos were driven by Christian values (for want of a better phrase). They were not all practicing Christians by any means, but they leaned toward the same definition of "good person" as defined by Christian thinking. Their needs were threefold. First, they needed to feel a direct connection with a fellow Australian who had fallen on hard times. Second, they needed to feel a direct connection with the Salvation Army officers, whom they respected. And third, they needed to experience a feeling of being a good person, this belief that they had done their duty by living according to their value set based on a Christian structure. This was not overtly religious, but it was an important aspect in meeting their needs.

It is difficult to work through the complexities of these donor needs if you work in an office, in middle management, or in senior leadership. People who worked at the headquarters of Salvos couldn't align on these needs; they simply couldn't grasp them.

You know who could? The Salvation Army officers.

These officers intuitively understood what the donor needed because they lived and breathed that reality. It was their truth. Every day, they had a direct connection with a fellow Australian in need, and they did their jobs because of this Christian value set. They knew exactly what the donor was looking for because it was what motivated them as well.

So in seminars, when Salvos would get bogged down, when they would introduce too much complexity, or when they couldn't agree, we would cut through the conflict by simply involving the Salvation Army officers. Their clarity reoriented the organization and brought it back to the important truths and helped the leadership understand the essence of what the organization was doing.

A diagram in Chapter 1 talked about service users at one end, donors at another, and the organization in the middle.

(continued)

(continued)

The best way of meeting donor needs is sometimes to take the organization out and connect the two. This is exactly what we saw with Salvos and why I find it so incredibly inspiring: just connect the donors with the Salvation Army officers and they will meet each other's needs extremely well.

Meeting reciprocal needs

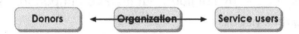

Figure 6.3 Meeting reciprocal needs.
Source: Revolutionise International Limited 2024.

Since culture is a big block of the Trifecta, let's look at another illustration about an organization that changed their culture with intent. Guide Dogs in the United Kingdom was one of our early clients. In Chapter 2, we saw how they arrived at their new ambition. How they changed their culture across the organization is equally legendary.

This was in the 2010s. Once Guide Dogs had finalized their new ambition and secured investment, they rolled out a massive training program on donor needs across the organization. Their focus for this program was emotional excellence. People who worked in training guide dogs, people who worked in training people with reduced sight to work with guide dogs, people in research and development, people who worked in finance and leadership – everyone, and I mean everyone – were taught how to recognize the emotional needs of donors and how to communicate to meet these needs. The nonprofit made an enormous investment at the time to train 200 of their staff in groups of 15. It paid off. After 10 years, they had increased their income by more than £50 million annually. Their investment in culture didn't even show as a rounding error in the scale of their new income.

This is what investing in culture and changing it with slow, careful intent can get you. It is a game changer.

Key Takeaways

I have a client, Şcoala Încrederii, that works across Romania to develop schools. Yesterday, they got a check from a bank to develop 15 schools within commuting distance of the bank's headquarters – a whopping €330 000, which is an incredible amount in Romania.

Talk about meeting donor needs.

To complete the Trifecta, you have to align the culture of your organization and bridge the cultural conflict. The best way to do this is to create a donor-conscious organization that focuses on "whole organization fundraising" – i.e. an organization that is as respectful of the donor and their needs as the fundraising department is and able to give fundraising what they need to meet those needs and be better than the competition at securing donors.

It seems so simple, but it is a fundamental change – and one that a lot of organizations shy away from. It is easy to see the point of the new ambition; it is powerful and inspiring. It is also relatively easy to see the value in the investment block; there are clear graphs that show the upside to thinking long-term. But culture is where most charities step back. Culture is scary. It is much harder to implement than investment and the new ambition because it does not have such hard, precise measurables. It is messy; it means bringing

(continued)

Culture and Ambition

(continued)

conflict out into the open and tackling it head-on, which can make leadership nervous. It involves convincing people, which is often purely emotional instead of clear and structural. Plus, it is a forever project. No wonder it seems daunting. No wonder people back off.

The key takeaway from this chapter is simply this: don't. We have shown you methods to introduce a cultural change in your organization, ways in which to do a soft or hard reset, and we have plenty of stories of charities that have done it successfully. But the key insight here is absolutely *don't give up*. Don't back off or walk away because it feels hard. If you stick with it, the upside is incredible.

And I don't just mean financially. I mean for everyone. How do you think a donor feels when their needs are met? Or an ethical intellectual when, six years later, they are able to help five times as many people because the nonprofit had more money? How do you think the fundraising team feels when they crush their targets because they have an organization that respects, supports, and enables them, or a service user feels when they receive help they couldn't get six years ago? Keep going. Everyone wins.

If you manage to implement all three blocks of the Trifecta, then you will be lined up and ready to trigger a Red Dot, that moment when a Great Fundraising Organization is focused and energized to accelerate growth. Part I has shown you the practical elements of a Red Dot – but, of course, there is a lot of nuance and conflict in executing this Trifecta and getting to that Red Dot. This nuance and conflict are why you must strive for emotional excellence. Let's discover how in Part II.

Part II

Striving for Emotional Excellence

Chapter 7

You Are in the Emotions Business

Over the last 20 years, I have grown more and more aware of the primacy of emotions in driving human behavior. The most beautiful lesson I've learned in these years is that the emotional needs of people around the world are exactly the same. There are cultural differences in how we cooperate, communicate, run our communities, or decide what is polite or acceptable behavior, but the basic human emotional drivers of people are the same everywhere.

For 99% of people, this includes the need to give, to contribute to the greater good.

The secret to being a great fundraiser is realizing that the profession is about helping people meet that need. That's it. I've known this for a long time, but the knowledge crystallized in a remarkable 24 hours in a remote place called Epupa.

Epupa is a tiny settlement on the banks of the Kunene River in Damaraland in northwestern Namibia. To get there, you spend several days driving in an offroad vehicle through a desert that was known for centuries as the Skeleton Coast. It is an exposed area and one of the least-developed places I've ever been. You have people there living in strong traditional communities in stunning surroundings, but there are also pockets of absolute poverty.

The drive up to Epupa was an experience in its own right. My family and I drove through barren land, completely isolated from other people and dependent on our four-wheel drive, which, in our case, was a Toyota Hilux with our tents strapped up top. I don't think I have ever felt so exposed and vulnerable.

Then the scenery changed. We moved from arid desert to this strip of lush river territory nestled along the rivers that form the arteries of central and southern Africa. Our campsite was beside a stunning waterfall on the Kunene River, and from looking at birds and desert creatures, suddenly we were spotting crocodiles and hippopotamuses. My seven-year-old son was beside himself with delight. This was his dream come true.

Once we were set up at the campsite, we commissioned a local guide to take us on a few hikes and show us the flora and fauna. Of course, these guides are phenomenal storytellers, and my family and I spent many pleasurable hours walking the territory and hearing stories about nature and how the people here folded it into their communities.

It turned out that this local guide, in addition to being a superb nature guide, was also a fantastic fundraiser. When we were enjoying a bitter lemon drink at the end of the hike, he told us about a village not very far away that belonged to the Himba people. The Himba people lived an extremely traditional way of life, and to visit their village would be an amazing cultural experience for us. But he also made the very strong case that these were people who needed our money. There was a drought in the region and the Himba people were suffering. I remember his line so clearly:

"These people have nothing," he said. "They need you to visit because this village does not even have one cow. They have no milk – there is nothing to drink."

The whole conversation took place through storytelling. Through stories and narrative, our guide showed us how much these people needed our money and that they were prepared to earn it by teaching us about their culture and therefore meeting our emotional needs. He showed us, clearly, that no one here was begging; the village had knowledge and a way of life that we would love to learn about, and our money, in turn, could help them keep that way of life. It was brilliantly done, all through dignified storytelling and a deep understanding of his audience. He was a natural, top-class fundraiser.

We couldn't visit the village in the end because we were short on time, but we left extra money with our guide to utilize how he saw fit. I have always believed this is fundraising in its most intrinsic, natural form: no organization, no structure or red tape, just somebody who was a successful member of his society understanding the emotional needs of his customers and the practical needs of the Himba people. It is still one of the best examples of fundraising I've seen.

Then a nine-year-old boy fell into the river.

A group of local boys had been playing underneath the waterfall when a nine-year-old boy disappeared. Immediately, the whole community came out to look for him. It obviously was not the first time this had happened because everyone knew what to do. It was a fast-flowing river, so the community was strung out along the banks for at least a kilometer, holding hands so that some people could wade into the water and search the river for him.

It was a beautifully organized and coordinated rescue, and it reminded me of one of our successful clients, the RNLI. The RNLI, of course, is in a different world, with different resources, equipment, and training, but it has exactly the same motivation: when one person gets into trouble with the water, volunteers will cooperate to do everything they can to rescue that individual.

Hours passed and the boy was not found. It was clear now that he had drowned; no one could survive this long in this river. So the community lined themselves along the riverbank for several kilometers downstream, with a person sitting every 100 meters or so, waiting patiently for the river to return the boy's body for funeral arrangements. They just sat there, waiting. It was one of the most humbling moments I have experienced.

The river must have returned the body in the middle of the night because we woke up to stars and drumming – deep, powerful, sustained drumming that marked the boy's funeral and the passing of his soul.

For the second time in 24 hours, I was privileged enough to see the deep human need of people to come together and save others. It was exactly the same emotional reaction I have seen in Lochinver, Scotland, or Saltash in Devon in the United Kingdom: the need of entire communities to support volunteers who are prepared to risk their lives to save others.

The difference, of course, is that in the United Kingdom, they have a massive fundraising organization – so they have the fastest boats, the best kits, the best navigation, the best materials, and the ability to educate people about what to do. Here, in one of the poorest places on the planet, the only thing the community had was their determination, cooperation, and generosity of spirit.

I cannot help but wonder: would they have saved that boy's life if they had the same equipment and facilities as the organizations in the United Kingdom do? The RNLI now has an expanding international program to prevent drowning globally. Maybe one day their expertise and influence will reach the Kunene River.

Fundraising changes the world. It gives us the opportunity to fix wrongs, to help those who need it, to shape a reality that is kinder, bigger, and better. It is never about begging for money; it is about earning it by meeting a basic and universal emotional need: our intrinsic desire to contribute. Almost all of us have it. Almost all of us want to help others and seek connection, to be part of something greater, to sit for hours by a riverside so we can perform the simple kindness of returning the body of a dead boy to his mother. It is what makes us human. We treasure it.

If you work in fundraising, then you are in the emotions business, whether you like it or not – and that is a good thing. Emotions are universal, and they are the primary drivers of action. The Great Fundraising Organizations know how to trigger a Red Dot, yes, but they also understand that the core of everything they do, the qualitative standard to which they must operate, is emotional excellence. If your nonprofit can accept this, if they can understand that meeting the donor's emotional need to contribute is a good thing in its own right – it makes people happy, helps them live congruent with their values, makes the world a better place – then your charity can climb to new heights.

This is the crux. This is the most difficult part of building a Great Fundraising Organization because it is one of the toughest things for nonfundraisers, and sometimes even fundraisers, to wrap their heads around. We have been told our whole professional lives to take the emotion out of our work. Now I am asking you to put it back in – and it won't be easy.

Prejudice Against Emotions

Ethical intellectuals – the professional development worker, the medical research professional – have spent their careers as scientists. They have been trained to use the scientific method of hypothesis, test, measure, and learn. Emotions don't feature in that method; in fact, they are considered a liability.

Fundraising, on the other hand, depends on emotions to be effective. It is about meeting that human, basic need to contribute and become part of something greater than oneself. It exists in an emotional space.

This creates a unique conundrum for nonprofits. On the one hand, you have professionals who have spent decades removing the emotion from their work. On the other hand, we turn up and say, "Hey, can you pop the emotion back in, please?" I'm not surprised we get a bad reaction.

But where does this resistance to emotion come from? We have identified four blocks to emotion in a nonprofit space:

- The fear of damaging an organization's service users
- The fear of manipulating people
- The fear of damaging an organization's credibility
- Distaste and discomfort

The first fear stems from the belief that emotions – or being "emotional" – disempowers people. The fear is that by using emotional stories to talk about a charity's work, the charity will end up painting their service users as weak, powerless, and pathetic.

The second fear is the belief that emotions can be manipulated and that by using stories to describe a charity's new ambition or purpose, the nonprofit is effectively weaponizing their service users' vulnerabilities to manipulate their donor's emotions. Neither, of course, paints the charity in a flattering light. If they stick to the facts, they believe, and tell those facts in a distant and dry manner, then they will be objective. But if they tell stories, then they are massaging the facts to tug at someone's heartstrings – and that is a cheap gimmick used by con artists.

The third fear is born from a very particular context. Ethical intellectuals interact with colleagues at conferences, where they are judged by the standards that all ethical intellectuals share: objectivity, testing, and evidence. The fear among many nonprofits is that if their peers see their external communications as being "overtly emotional," they will be criticized for it, and it will damage the organization's credibility.

The last fear, that of distaste and discomfort, is understandable. It is natural to be uncomfortable about emotions when you have been trained in your professional career to guard against them.

Put these four fears together and you have the general reaction we face when we ask nonprofits to introduce emotion into their work: shock, disbelief, and then strong opposition. Most people are convinced you cannot work in an emotional space with integrity – and if it cannot be done with integrity, then it should not be done at all.

Truth Well-Told

Yet, meeting your donor's emotional needs is the heart and soul of good fundraising, and it *can* be done with integrity. We usually work with organizations across days to train them to work with emotions and to demonstrate to them how, through research, practice, and hard work, it is possible to meet emotional needs with integrity. For this book, I'll give you the short version. The solution to all four of the prejudices above can be summed up in three words:

Truth well-told.

Have you ever watched a video called *Free Solo*? It is a tape of Alex Honnold, the first man to climb El Capitan in Yosemite without a rope. There is a moment in that video that is so famous now it has its own name: the boulder problem. Alex is 2,000 ft above ground. In order to move forward, he has to do a karate kick or a two-legged jump along the cliff face, with only his thumbs as points of contact. This is the crux of his climb. It is the single point in time that defines the whole path. If he makes the move without dying, he makes it to the top. If he fails, he falls.

Understanding the "truth well-told" is like this crux. Your organization gets it and you move to the top. If it doesn't, you fall.

A truth well-told is the ability to describe the problem you are facing with honesty and integrity while keeping its emotional core intact. There is, of course, a problem you are facing; if there wasn't, you would not be fundraising for more money. When you concentrate on communicating a truth well-told, you focus on describing that problem as honestly and as powerfully as you can to connect with your donors. Integrity in fundraising means telling the "truth." Emotional excellence in fundraising means ensuring it is "well-told."

So how does the concept of a truth well-told answer each of the prejudices against emotions that we have described earlier? Let's take the first fear, that an emotional story will present a charity's service users as weak and pathetic. The answer to this is to let service users tell their own stories. Empower them; let them describe the problem in their own words. It is the best way to get the truth. Nine times out of 10, a service user will state the problem more precisely and more powerfully than the professionals will.

The second fear is the belief that emotional storytelling can manipulate a person. But the truth is you cannot manipulate a person's emotions if you tell the truth. People build up their emotional history through natural selection and life experiences, and there is nothing you can do to change that. This is why not everyone donates to every cause. All you can do is tell a story that is rooted in integrity and honesty – a truth well-told – and people with the matching emotional experience will react to that story. You cannot control emotions. You can only activate them.

The third fear, about organizational credibility, is linked closely to organizational vulnerability. Every charity wants to demonstrate that they are good at what they do – who wouldn't? – but the organizations that get it right show that they are not good *enough* at what they do. Not yet. The problem they are trying to solve still exists in the world, which is why they need more money: to save more people. To acknowledge this is to acknowledge an organizational vulnerability; it is what we called, in Chapter 4, an uncomfortable truth. But it is absolutely *the truth*, and your job as a charity is to own it, to communicate that truth powerfully so you can do good in the world. Saying you have not saved everyone as yet does not make you a failing nonprofit. It makes you a driven, powerful organization that won't stop until your purpose, no matter how audacious or incredible, is achieved.

Lastly, ethical intellectuals react to emotions with distaste and discomfort, which is why they shy away from it. Their fear is people will have similar reactions to emotional storytelling, this sense of *Why are you telling me this? This makes me uncomfortable; I don't want to hear it.*

Honestly, though, that is the point. People should find the continued existence of these problems distasteful and uncomfortable. What do comfortable people do? Nothing. If we are not uncomfortable in the face of a distasteful truth, then we are no longer human. Tell the donor a truth well-told. Make them uncomfortable. Show them how their actions can connect to their emotional needs and help change the world.

The Science of Storytelling: Focus Your Emotion

A common misconception among people is that emotions are subjective and therefore antithetical to the scientific method and to objectivity. But the truth is working in an emotional space *is* a science; it is just a behavioral science, which is a different science from what many of us know. People are illogical, but they are predictable. You can measure, test, and implement behavioral science.

In fact, to work effectively in an emotional space, you must be incredibly precise. It is not enough to have emotion in your fundraising communications. You must focus that emotion to connect with people who have the correct emotional history. Remember how we said emotions cannot be manipulated? This means you have to find the right donors for you, the people whose emotional experience and needs align with the problem your organization is trying to solve. To do that, you have to insert the right emotion into your fundraising communications to activate their emotional past.

This is simple, but it is not easy. It takes a lot more effort and cooperation than anyone imagined to ascertain that precise and differentiating emotional focus. The one tool we have at our disposal to achieve this breakthrough is the organization's stories.

The emotional focus of a nonprofit is in the collective power of their stories – stories of the service users they have worked with and the service users they haven't worked with yet, stories of donors, supporters, volunteers, founders, staff. Gather those stories together and you will find the emotional power of a nonprofit, running like a quiet river underneath the narratives, a distinct and clear voice that attracts the right donors to the organization.

Human beings are genetically predisposed to react to stories. This is not an analogy. It is in our DNA. It has been there for a long time, and it is genetically hardwired into us to keep us safe. How? In ancient times, when we gathered around a fire and told stories about the moon, the sun, big beasts, and bad people, we were teaching the community about what would help them survive and what would kill them. Oral traditions were humanity's way of passing on knowledge, of teaching the next generation how to live in the world effectively. Those who emotionally reacted to the stories survived. Those who didn't, died, which means we now have a population that is genetically hardwired to pay attention when you tell them a narrative.

Every ancient culture has a rich tradition of oral storytelling. It is in the Celtic culture, in the songline tradition of the Aboriginal people, in the stories of the Native Americans, in the many cultures of India and South Africa. Stories have been our guiding lights since the beginning of time. We listen to stories; we cannot help it. This is why it is not a choice to work with the science of storytelling or in an emotional space. It is an imperative.

Find Your Magic

So how do you get an organization to accept the primacy of emotion in fundraising, to agree on how they focus their emotion, and to free up the fundraising team to move forward?

The honest answer is that it takes work, mutual respect, and cocreation. It circles back to what we spoke about in Chapter 1: acceptance that, in order to become a Great Fundraising Organization, you are in fact two businesses in one, and one of those businesses must strive toward meeting the emotional needs of your donors. Your organization must learn to respect emotions as a science and acknowledge their power in driving behavior.

You must also accept that you cannot *think* emotionally. You can only work in an emotional space. Many people email me to ask, "Alan, we don't have a big budget. Could you do one online seminar and teach us how to think more emotionally?" I cannot because thinking does not work in an emotional space; you can only live it. The best tried and tested methodology for working with emotions is to immerse yourself in the emotional space and wait until the magic pops.

People don't believe me when I tell them this. They always think there must be a faster, slicker method to getting emotions right. Others panic. *What do you mean you have to wait around till the magic pops? Where is the structure? The to-do list? The proven storytelling format?*

This panic can make people do strange things. I had an organization once that listened to my seminars, took notes on how to work in an emotional space, and then went away for a year to focus their emotional storytelling. When they came back, they said, "We have decided to write all of our fundraising communications in the format of a hero's journey, and in every story, our organization will be the hero."

It was such a terrible idea, I had to walk away from the project. They had ignored organizational vulnerability. They had ignored an uncomfortable truth. They had even turned their back on a truth well-told. They were so determined to get the storytelling right and were so lost without guardrails that they chose the worst narrative structure as a format.

It is an important story, though, because it speaks to a common preconception about storytelling. People believe narratives are prescriptive structures and that if they can just choose an established storytelling structure, they will automatically access an emotional space. What I am asking of you is more honest, true, and raw than that. I am asking you to sit with your stories, to exist in that space no matter how uncomfortable it becomes or how long it takes, until you can see that magic spark, that differentiating emotional focus, emerge.

To do this, you have to be extremely insightful, very open-minded, and courageous enough to act when that magic pops out.

Illustration: WSPA[*], United Kingdom, and Never Alone, Romania

In 2009, during the last days of my agency career, I got into a bit of a standoff with an old client, the World Society for the Protection of Animals United Kingdom (WSPA). WSPA had been a successful client of ours for almost a decade, but after we merged with another agency, the relationship and the results started to go south. It got so bad I was called in to see the international marketing director, a

---

[*] Please note that some years after this casework happened, WSPA rebranded and relaunched as World Animal Protection with a different communications strategy.

very talented man, Phil Woollam. I went to that meeting expecting to be fired. I had no hope of saving the account but only wanted to close off a valuable relationship with dignity.

Phil, who is wonderfully direct, asked me what was going wrong. I told him we were not being briefed correctly. We had 10 years' worth of evidence on what worked, but we were briefed the opposite, so much so that it was almost unethical for us to keep taking these briefs because we knew they couldn't succeed. So Phil told us to get his team and my team into a room and just work this out. We would explain our evidence to his team so they knew where we were coming from, and we would get everyone on the same page.

"I'd love to do that, Phil," I said, "but I can't. My team won't do it. They are terrified of being blamed for contradicting the client and losing the account."

"You won't lose the account," he said. "You have my word. Do whatever it takes to get this aligned."

So for the first time ever, we got everyone in a room to work unplugged – and, oh boy, was this some seminar. We went hard. We were utterly uncompromising. So were the client team. There were tears. There were people storming out. In the late afternoon, we had to calm everyone down. At one point, the client told me, "Alan, you are *really* pissing me off."

"Good!" I said. "That's what I want to do. Because we're sitting here in this intellectual blancmange going round and round in circles, and I want to unlock the anger in your organization. Because if we don't, we're never going to unlock growth."

"Wait," someone else said. "Do you think we're an *angry* organization?"

(continued)

153

You Are in the Emotions Business

(continued)

"Yes, I do! I've got years' worth of evidence that suggests there are two types of people who give to animal charities. There are people who like cute, cuddly animals—the dogs, the cats, the hamsters—and want to care for them, so they donate to their local charities. The people who donate to organizations like yours—the international nonprofits, the ones that focus on animal rights— these people are *angry*. They are angry that evil human beings exist who will torture animals for profit or pleasure, and they want you to do something about it. They want you to express their anger somehow and put a stop to that cruelty."

Immediately, there were protests – *of course WSPA wasn't an angry organization!* – but the United Kingdom director of fundraising, Rosie Chinchen, cut in. "It's absolutely right," she said quietly. "Our donors feel angry. They are furious at people acting out injustices on animals, and they want us to put it right."

The international fundraising director, Simon Batten, backed her up. It was an uncomfortable truth, but we had taken the first step toward acknowledging it. Someone wrote out W S P A in large letters on the whiteboard and then added a word next to each letter: *We Sell Powerful Anger*. The sentence clicked. This was it. This was what WSPA did. Now all they had to do was find a way to communicate this. The word "powerful" was crucial. WSPA gave the donors the ability and power to act on their anger by doing something constructive, thus precisely meeting their needs.

After that, there were no more logical analyses about animal rights, the theory of change, or a structural rights framework. It became an entire day of storytelling. Members of the WSPA team told stories about how people all over the world solved the problem of animal cruelty using their donors' money. They moved away from case studies and focused on emotion, on how their staff felt when they came back from fieldwork, on what they were up against. It was utterly amazing.

The project was picked up to pilot in the United Kingdom, after which it was rolled out globally. The person on point charged with delivering the project was Kerry Vandersypen (who readers will notice is now the second-longest serving person at Revolutionise), and it was a phenomenal success. WSPA focused on "We sell powerful anger," and it created a manifold increase in revenue. In the year that "powerful anger" was launched, the United Kingdom team saw a revenue increase of 235%. The CEO of WSPA publicly thanked Kerry, Rosie, and the fundraising team for reversing the financial fortunes of a fundraising program in decline.

My work with WSPA changed how I understood fundraising. It was the first time we got to drive strategy based on a single emotional insight rather than a long, overly logical briefing, and it pulled the veil back on how instrumental emotions are to what we do as fundraisers. We are in the emotions business, no question about it.

I find emotions especially powerful to work with because although they are universal drivers of behavior, they also connect in unique cultural and historical ways to specific populations, opening out the potential for nuance. An excellent illustration of this is Never Alone in Romania, a charity that seeks to tackle loneliness and isolation among the elderly in the country.

Now, it is notoriously difficult to raise money to combat loneliness among the elderly as a cause, but Romania's population had a unique differentiator. Usually, in more mature economies, the old people have most of the wealth while the young people have less. Romania's economy, however, was upside down. Due to the

(continued)

(continued)

country's history and political upheaval, it was actually the young who were wealthy and the elderly who were poor. The youth had reaped the benefits of technology and an increasing number of opportunities in a globalized world, while the older population had been left behind.

Never Alone understood this insight. They knew the youth in Romania were likely proud of their generation's achievements as well as felt a sense of responsibility for the generation above them that lost out on this growth. Never Alone focused on the elderly telling their own stories – on how it felt to be left behind, to watch an economic boom flower after their prime because of the country's history, to feel isolated, alone, and forgotten. It was remarkably powerful and led to revolutionary fundraising growth. Never Alone kept emotion at the core of their fundraising effort, but they recognized how activating emotion depended on the unique cultural and political history of the people they were speaking to and about.

Key Takeaways

Almost every person has a deep and basic human need to give. Fundraising earns its money by meeting that need. To become a Great Fundraising Organization, you must recognize and accept you are in the emotions business – and that's a good thing.

So many of our clients struggle with this. It is often the core conflict across the organization: the reluctance to work in an emotional space, to meet donor's emotional needs, and therefore to give fundraising the freedom and the materials they require to truly succeed. There is an entrenched prejudice against emotions, a belief that they damage an organization's credibility, their service users' dignity, and everyone's integrity.

But it is absolutely possible to meet your donor's emotional needs with integrity if you are prepared to work hard at it. This means not just accepting but treasuring the unique emotional need that your organization exists to fulfill among your donors. It means respecting the power of emotions, their primacy in driving human behavior, and their status as a science. The best way I have of framing it is *emotions are why we do things; logic is why we don't do stupid things*. To become a Great Fundraising Organization, you must accept you are working with behavioral science, and that is about predictability, not logic.

I know this can be a deeply uncomfortable process, but I also urge you to remember that that is the point. Comfortable people don't take action. Uncomfortable people create change, especially when what is making them uncomfortable is a distasteful injustice in the world. Look for your uncomfortable truth, that problem you haven't solved as yet. Sit with the discomfort it evokes in you, the rage, the sadness, the pain. Harness it. The Great Fundraising Organizations are exquisite storytellers. Tell your story with your whole heart.

Chapter 8

Identifying Donor Needs

Merseyside is a region in the United Kingdom, with the River Mersey running through it. On one side of the river is Liverpool. On the other is the Wirral.

The Wirral is home to Claire House Children's Hospice, which was, at the time, a moderately successful fundraising organization. In 2014, they found themselves with a specific, unfulfilled need: their services were not reaching many of the families that needed them across Merseyside. At that point, they were developing strategic plans to grow, but the only way to reach those families was to expand their services. To do so, they needed increased fundraising revenue.

The problem with Claire House Children's Hospice – and it will be a familiar problem to you by now – was that there was an aversion to fundraising on the clinical and social sides of the nonprofit. The medical professionals felt it was a bit demeaning to fundraise, and they were disengaged from it. There was a political point of view that organizations such as children's hospices shouldn't be forced to fundraise at all because the government should be funding care for the critically ill (which is, to a major extent, valid). And there were the usual objections: a dislike of emotion, fear that their service users would not want Claire House to tell their stories, concerns that fundraising communications would damage the credibility of the organization, etc.

There was no open hostility. No one was dismissive of the fundraising team or rude. The rest of the organization just couldn't get to a place where they understood how fundraising worked. They understood the need for the money, but they couldn't envision a fundraising process that safeguarded the organization's integrity or the integrity of their service users.

To an extent, the fundraising team was also stumped. A junior member of the team, who had just joined Claire House Children's Hospice's fundraising team, put it like this: in her previous job, fundraising was straightforward. She was raising money to help sick people, which meant she could make a simple promise to the donor: give us money and a sick person will get better.

But at Claire House, she couldn't make that promise. People did send money to Claire House, but there was no hope that their money would make the children better. "I don't understand," she said. "Who is being healed?"

It was a pivotal word: *healed*. We were all together in a room at this point: the fundraising team, members of the trustee board, the medical professionals, the services departments, everyone who had the power to create organization-wide change. It was the CEO of Claire House, David Pastor, who had got us here. He is a high-energy talent, a real powerhouse, and he knew the nonprofit needed to be in a single space to work through its key conflicts. For hours now, we had been circling the problem, trying to find a way in which fundraising could be both effective and operate with integrity.

Then came this word "healed."

It was a senior nurse who answered. She was thinking out loud, working through the problem. "Well, the child's life is better for sure," she said. "But you're right – often we can't save them, no matter how much we want to. So I suppose, ultimately, we're healing the moms and dads, the brothers and sisters, extended family, school friends. We're healing the community."

Then she paused and looked out the window, as the moment dawned on her clearly. "My goodness," she said. "Fundraising helps to heal the people my team cannot reach. We're all on the same side."

It was true. The death of a child shatters the whole community. Everyone would do anything to save that life, but it isn't always possible to heal someone from illness. There is often nothing they can do. So they make a donation to a hospice. It is the only outlet for their grief and powerlessness, the one way in which they can make a difference.

It was the breakthrough that changed the organization's perspective on fundraising. Fundraising was not distasteful or demeaning; it was not begging. Fundraising helped serve a need in people. It was a powerful, honorable act in its own right.

Soon after, Claire House Children's Hospice rolled out fundraising communications with inspired stories. I will never forget the story of Jack, a boy who died at the hospice. It was a simple truth, well told, with dignity, detail, and permission from Jack's family. Ten years later, Claire House now provides services for everyone in Merseyside who needs them. They achieved this by more than doubling their fundraising income.

Claire House Children's Hospice

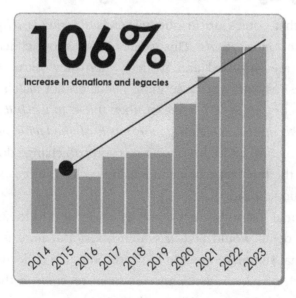

Figure 8.1 Claire House Children's Hospice growth chart.
Source: Revolutionise International Limited 2024.

Identifying Donor Needs

In the last chapter, we talked about recognizing that donors have a fundamental, human need to give and that the job of fundraising is to earn money by meeting that need. In this chapter, let's examine this with deeper nuance. You can peel this fundamental human need to give into multiple layers, dividing across country, culture, demographics, and interests. In other words, different people need to give to support different causes. A Great Fundraising Organization identifies the people who have a need to support their unique cause and then focuses their fundraising communications on those donors. For Claire House Children's Hospice, it was people who needed to heal their grief and powerlessness by donating to the organization. For your nonprofit, it will be something else.

People need to give – that is a fact. Your job is to find out what those needs are and which ones align with your organization's purpose.

Identifying Versus Changing Needs

A refrain that comes up in our masterclass series is *why can't we change our donor's needs?* This usually comes from ethical intellectuals who are surprised and baffled when they learn about their donors' desires, partly because those needs do not match what they were expecting. *It would be easier*, they think, *to teach the donor to want something else, something more easily aligned with our purpose.*

The short answer to this question is you *can* change donor needs but not in the timeframe of a fundraising cycle. The reason is a person's emotional history.

Emotional histories are a complex topic, and to focus on them in proper detail would take a whole book. But here is a simple, foundational summary: people move through life collecting experiences, each of which elicits an emotional reaction in them, along with a thought pattern. Those thought patterns and emotional reactions become linked, forming what we call an emotional history. People's emotional histories are vital because firstly, as we know, emotions drive behavior. Secondly, those histories shape a person's value system, which is especially relevant for fundraising in the nonprofit sector.

Think of these histories as hardwired into us by experience. You cannot change a person's emotional history – and therefore their value system – with a single advertising campaign. It has taken thousands of experiences and tens of thousands of hours to build up this history; it is not going to morph with one advert.

The only way to change one's emotional history is by practice. Lots and lots of practice – tens of thousands of hours, if not more. Anyone who has been in a personal recovery program or has done therapy will attest to this. It takes time.

There are a few nonprofits that understand this, and they have set out to deliberately change their donors' values. Greenpeace is a famous example. They have spent decades trying to develop people's values so that people will care more about nature and the planet. Many of their big campaigns were planned, and have lasted, for 20–25 years because they knew how long it takes to see a significant value shift.

Most fundraising departments do not operate with this kind of timeline. Fundraising works best in the long-term, yes, but we are talking about timescales of 5, 7, or 10 years. The campaigning side of a nonprofit can be excellent at changing people's values across two decades, but evidence shows it is difficult to achieve this in a shorter time period.

The best you can do to trigger the Red Dot is *identify* people who already have the values, and therefore the emotional histories, that align with your organization and then communicate with them with precision. All our research has come to the same conclusion: it is best to meet the donor where they are right now.

163

Identifying Donor Needs

When we talk about values and timescales, I'm always reminded of *Blue Peter*. *Blue Peter* is a famous television program in the United Kingdom targeted toward young teenagers; I grew up watching it, and I know many in my generation who did too. Every year, *Blue Peter* did a charity appeal, where they featured nonprofits such as the RNLI and Guide Dogs.

Forty years later, I am now at a time in my life where I have money to give. Who do my generation habitually and automatically give to? The RNLI and Guide Dogs. I call them our "Pavlovian charities" because people in my generation in the United Kingdom instinctively give money to them. They *are* excellent charities, but the reason they are our Pavlovian charities is because when we were teenagers, when our values were still forming, a television program we trusted told us they were good. Forty years later, our emotional history and value system have not changed. The only difference now is we have more money to give.

Why People Give

In the last chapter, we examined how almost everyone has a fundamental human need to contribute. But what are the big-picture, macro reasons why people give? What drives us?

Healing

In the biggest picture, giving is often a form of healing. A person's emotional makeup is shaped by their emotional history, and therefore their need to give is predominantly shaped by their life story and the neural networks created by their memories that guide their emotional responses and good behavior. Thus, people often give to heal an experience that has been hurtful or uncomfortable. It could be an experience they lived through or an experience they witnessed secondhand through travel, friends, or the news; it could be any association with fear or loss. Research now shows that people who donate to combat global acts of terrorism or the climate crisis do so because they are traumatized by those experiences, whether on a minor or major scale, and they are healing their sense of fright by giving.

Happiness

According to research, giving is always associated with a sense of happiness. By "happiness," we don't mean the ecstatic joy that people so often confuse with happiness but a simple, inner peace, a sense of contentment that comes from living in a way that is congruent with one's values.

Self-Esteem

Ninety-nine percent of the world's population draws their self-esteem from their ability to contribute. (There is 1% that gets their self-esteem in other ways, but don't focus on them in your fundraising, no matter how much attention they demand.) If all we can do is take and receive, we lose our sense of self-worth. If, however, we can contribute, then we build up a feeling of self-respect.

It is no coincidence that if you look at any organized program aimed at human happiness, the final step of the program is to give. Consider the NHS's Five Steps to Mental Wellbeing:

1. Connect with other people

2. Be physically active

3. Learn new skills

4. Pay attention to the present moment

5. Give to others

Even the twelfth step of Alcoholics Anonymous is to help the next person; helping someone overcome their addiction is a way to strengthen your own sobriety. As I write this, I am almost 10 years into recovery from my alcohol addiction, and I am currently sponsoring a young man in his first year of battle. He sent me a text this morning saying, "For the first time in a decade, I am happy." It gave me an immense sense of peace.

To whom and how we contribute differs from person to person. Some people are happy contributing to their inner circles: their families, their neighborhoods, the local church or community. Others need to feel like they are contributing on a global scale: to world peace, to end global hunger, or to save the natural world. Different causes interact with our emotional histories and values differently, which is why people need to give in different ways to create their sense of self-esteem.

Connection

People also donate to feel connected to likeminded people with whom they share an emotional history, which strengthens their sense of belonging. The need for connection is huge in wealthy countries at the moment, but it is largely unrecognized in fundraising. We assume people give money to organizations, but this isn't true – people give to people because they crave connection. Think of the Greek root of the word "philanthropy," which, when translated, means "loving people." For more data and analysis on love and connection in fundraising, see Professor Jen Shang's work on philanthropic psychology (and her excellent organization, the Institute for Sustainable Philanthropy), which evidences that love is the driver for most charitable giving.

Meaningful Life

I don't think it is an exaggeration to say that a lifetime of giving adds greatly to this sense of a life well-lived and a life lived with meaning.

Research shows that when donors leave a legacy gift in their will for a charity, it is often this feeling that spurs them. As people get older, some of them are fortunate enough to collect assets and disposable income. Gifting some of those assets to solve a problem that you truly care about can give your life and hard work meaning. It can make much of one's life worthwhile.

When Giles Pegram worked as director for the NSPCC, he dealt with many high-net-worth individuals for donations. He worked closely with them over a long period to educate them about the organization, showcase NSPCC's work, and gain their trust. When it came time to solicit a large donation, simply asking "Will you please donate?" was nowhere near as effective as saying, "Thank you for your time. You have now come to know us, the problem we are solving, and I hope you have come to respect our projects and trust our policies and our people. I am here today because I think right now is your chance to do something truly extraordinary. A game-changing gift to the NSPCC will alter the landscape of what is possible, and your donation will have made that happen. This is what we are giving to you: a chance to make a world-altering difference. This is what you are giving to us . . ." and he went on to explain how their donation would be used by the charity.

By explaining to the donors what *they* would get out of contributing, Pegram addressed his donors' needs, whether they understood it or not. He was giving them a chance to do something meaningful, and it changed the ask.

Identifying Your Donors

So if different people contribute to different causes for various and often surprising reasons, how does an organization go about identifying their correct donor base and then discovering their needs?

The first step is to recognize that the people who give your nonprofit money are not the same kind of people who work within your organization. Your donor's emotional history will likely differ from that of your staff; occasionally, there is overlap, but generally it is starkly different. We recommend that every organization we work with put up a sign at their offices: *You Are Not the Audience.* It reminds people who work at the nonprofit that while their emotional reactions and thoughts on fundraising communications are respected, they are not the target audience. Those communications are not designed for them.

The second step is to find and target people who need to support your nonprofit's mission for any of the five reasons we mentioned above (healing, happiness, self-esteem, connection, and meaning of life). This means searching for those people whose emotional history already aligns with your organization's purpose and who are looking to solve the same problem as you.

Ideally, you want to work in the space where the "why" of the nonprofit intersects with the "why" of the donor. Our data has shown that if an organization can focus their fundraising efforts in that unique space, and continue working in that space with discipline, then they unlock growth.

But why is working in that space so vital? Because it is here that you find two key segments of the population: what we call the "always" and the "maybes."

In any fundraising market, the population – whether it is five million in Finland or a billion in India – can be split into three segments. The largest segment is what we call the "nevers." These are people who will never give to your organization, not because they are mean-spirited or do not want to contribute but simply because their emotional history does not align with your nonprofit's cause. The second segment is the "maybes." These are people who might give to your

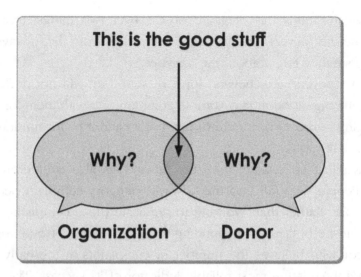

Figure 8.2 The space where the "why" of the nonprofit intersects with the "why" of the donor.
Source: Revolutionise International Limited 2024.

organization but have not as yet. They have the right emotional history, but you have not communicated with them properly to activate their emotions. And lastly, there are the "always." These are people who will always donate to your organization no matter how you communicate or what you send them because they are habituated to donate to your nonprofit.

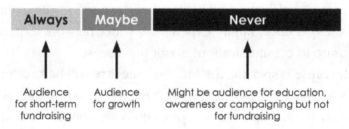

Figure 8.3 Always, maybes, and nevers.
Source: Revolutionise International Limited 2024.

Identifying Donor Needs

Organizations that stagnate obsess over two things: trying to educate the "nevers" and avoiding complaints from the "always." In doing so, they forget about the "maybes."

The "nevers" are "nevers" for a reason: they will not donate to you. The organization may want to communicate with them for campaigning purposes or for education, but it cannot be for fundraising. There is no point.

Avoiding complaints from the "always" is also counterproductive. People who fall into the "always" category complain because they care. Rather than working to eradicate those complaints, it is better to be brilliant at responding to them. I know of one appeals director who believes the number of complaints in the early days of an appeal is the most reliable indicator of its success. The more complaints, the more people care, the more successful the appeal is. He simply focuses his energy on ensuring his team is brilliant at managing and responding to those complaints.

What most organizations miss and the Great Fundraising Organizations actively focus on is their "maybes." Fundraising profit comes from brilliant communication to the "always," but fundraising *growth* comes from correct communication to the "maybes."

The size of the "maybe" market depends on how many people have an emotional experience with your nonprofit's cause. Cancer, for example, has a big "maybe" segment because almost everyone has an emotional history with the word "cancer" – either through personal experience, family experience, wider network experience, or exposure to communications about the disease.

If the cause is specific, the "maybe" category will be smaller. Leprosy, for example, does not have as large a "maybe" market as cancer. But, as the Leprosy Mission powerfully demonstrated, a smaller market can be high in value. The people in the "maybe" segment for leprosy tend to be Christian, as eradicating leprosy is what Jesus preached in the Bible. This means you have a very small but very focused segment that knows two things: one, leprosy still exists, and two, eradicating it is part of their core values. If you can activate that segment, it can be tremendously powerful.

Evidence shows that focusing on the "maybes" and communicating with them with precision leads to fundraising growth. They are the segment you should keep your eyes on; they live in that unique space where the "why" of the nonprofit and the "why" of the donor intersect.

Identifying Your Donor's Needs

Once you have identified your "always" and "maybe" markets, it is imperative to *distinguish* your organization within those markets. Here, we are diving deeper into the uniqueness of the need you are fulfilling. What specific itch are you scratching for your donor as an organization? Why should the "maybes" give their money to you instead of another charity tackling a similar cause?

I want to be clear: this section is not about how to target your "maybe" segment from a marketing lens. This book is not about good external marketing. Our focus is on getting the people *within* your organization to agree on your donor profile and your donor's needs. We are seeking internal alignment and consensus that helps the fundraising department streamline toward meeting the donor's wants.

There are a number of tools that can help you discover more about the donors in your "maybe" segment and learn about the nuances of their desires. We prefer three tools: the psychographic model, the biology model, and the identity model. Each of these tools is a different way of looking at and structuring the big five macro reasons we discussed earlier in the chapter (in section "Why People Give").

Psychographic Model

For complex and larger organizations, we prefer a psychographic model. It is more useful to know what people need rather than just

171

who they are. The model we use was created for us by Cultural Dynamics Strategy and Marketing. Cultural Dynamics worked with a model of 108 basic human values that they conglomerated into segments and cohorts, after which we collaborated with them to develop our proprietary model.

According to this model, the donor population divides into three main segments:

- The dutiful faithful
- The ambitious achievers
- The ethical intellectuals

Each of these segments further divides into two:

- The dutiful faithful = My tribe + Follow the leader
- The ambitious achievers = Look cool + Act fast
- The ethical intellectuals = Experimenters + Be right

To drive fundraising growth, we generally focus on four segments: "my tribe," "follow the leader," "act fast," and "experimenters." These donors are more focused on the actions they take, as opposed to the "look cool" and "be right" segments who are more concerned about what people think.

When we use the psychographic model, we throw a question at the millions of data points in this database and get an answer as to which type of person supports which cause with greater than 95% certainty.

Below is a graph from this model featuring people who donate to animal charities. As you can see, they predominantly fall into four categories: "experimenters," "be right," "my tribe," and "follow the leader."

Now look at the chart for people who donate to children's and youth charities.

Animal charities

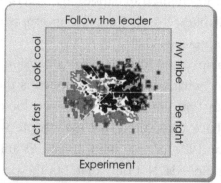

Figure 8.4 Animal charities.

Source: Reprinted with permission from Cultural Dynamics Strategy & Marketing Ltd., 2003–2024. All rights reserved.

Children and youth charities

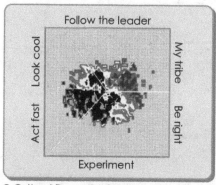

Figure 8.5 Children and youth charities.

Source: Reprinted with permission from Cultural Dynamics Strategy & Marketing Ltd., 2003–2024. All rights reserved.

It is interesting that, with the exception of the "experimenters," people who give to children's charities are everyone who does not give to animal charities. It is the "act fast" group, which is noticeably missing from the previous chart.

There are complicated reasons for this division that we will not get into here, but what I want you to notice is the level of differentiation you can find among donors if you look carefully. From two charts, we have discovered that the people who give to children's charities and the people who donate to animal charities do not have the same needs. Not only that, but the people who give to different animal charities are different from *each other* when it comes to why and how they give.

This information is powerful for differentiating your organization and identifying those specific needs that your nonprofit can uniquely meet. For example, here is a graph on people who donate to armed forces charities.

Armed forces charities

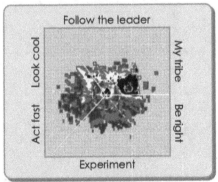

Figure 8.6 Armed forces charities.
Source: Reprinted with permission from Cultural Dynamics Strategy & Marketing Ltd., 2003–2024. All rights reserved.

It is predominately "my tribe," i.e. people who focus on direct connection. This is what the armed forces are about: belonging to a group, that famous comradery or mateship that keeps people safe and gives them the courage to act bravely in horrific and challenging circumstances.

Based on this insight, we created a purpose and new ambition with the Soldiers', Sailors', and Airmen's Families Association (SSAFA), the armed forces charity in the United Kingdom that provides services to people who are in or coming out of the Army, Navy, or Air Force, and their families, who are struggling emotionally and physically. These same people, while they were in service, were surrounded by likeminded peers who offered them support and comradery. Once they left service, however, they found themselves facing a whole host of problems in the new world, with no support structure and often with the additional burden of emotional trauma from their time in combat. They were utterly alone, and they were missing the connection that they relied on when in service.

So we came up with a very simple new ambition with SSAFA: "Never battle alone." These are three words that bring together the precise needs of the service user *and* the donor.

Biological Model

The psychographic model is fantastic but complex, and it does not always suit an organization's needs. For some charities, we use the biological model, which focuses on the four different reasons why we give, based on our evolution.

The first is the basic physical empathy that we share with every other animal species, and that demands a feeling of one-to-one connection. For donors, this means that they need to feel like they are helping a fellow human being in need, not just solving an abstract problem.

The second is cooperation, which is the human need to know that we are connected with other people in trying to solve a common problem or injustice. It is the same motivation behind the concept of "pay it forward."

The third is esteem: the donor needs to feel good about themselves through the act of giving, either internally (*I am a good person because I am living life in congruence with my values*) or externally (*I look like a good person because I am helping others*).

The last is sacrifice. There is a biological need to exist in groups with people who are prepared to take risks, be brave, and if necessary, sacrifice themselves for the common good. We admire bravery and sacrifice and those who are capable of it. This is a category that drives many charities, such as military nonprofits or, for example, the RNLI, whose donors admire the courage of the volunteer crew.

Identity Model

This is the simplest model we use, and it was driven by the groundbreaking work of the world's first philanthropic psychologist, Professor Jen Shang, supported and accompanied by her husband, Professor Adrian Sargeant. According to Professor Shang, people can express or even develop their identity through repeated donations. They are not just donating to a charity; they are expressing and creating their sense of self through those donations.

Using this insight, there are two questions that members of a nonprofit can think about when trying to understand their donors:

- What is the donor saying about themselves by giving to this organization?
- After the donor has made the gift, how do they feel about themselves?

This is a brilliant internal tool to help the organization's staff step into the minds of their donors; it helps them empathize and start to feel like donors. It brings them closer to discovering their donors' identities and caring for them as people, not just someone who gives.

Through a four-year longitudinal study, Professor Shang and her team have now evidenced that if an organization is able to meet their donors' needs across the long-term, then the nonprofit doubles their income *as well as* increases the well-being of their donors. Meeting donor needs truly is a win-win.

Illustration: Scottish Book Trust, Scotland

One of the best examples I have seen of identifying one's donors and targeting their needs is the Scottish Book Trust. I love this organization because when my son was very young, the Scottish Book Trust surprised my wife with a present of books for him. We all live in Scotland, but my wife is Danish, so this came as a surprise to her.

"We don't get this in Denmark!" she told me.

"Well," I said, "welcome to the Enlightenment." We both laughed our heads off.

The Scottish Book Trust is smaller than several organizations we work with because it is operating in a smaller country, but it is dominant in its market. It promotes books and reading across Scotland through mobile libraries, volunteer services, literacy and writing services, as well as work in prisons. It is an incredible organization.

A few years ago, the organization wanted to address a specific problem that concerned them greatly: a reduction in the number

(continued)

(continued)

of parents who read books to children at bedtime. This is traditionally one of the famous bonding experiences between parents and their child, and I speak from personal experience when I say playing on a Nintendo does not substitute for reading a story to your child before bedtime.

When the Scottish Book Trust looked deeper into the problem, they found two reasons for the reduction. The first was the rise in the dominance of electronic mediums, such as online videos and television. The second was more shocking: the widening wealth gap.

Since 2008, the poor in Scotland have been growing desperately poor, while the rich have been getting wealthier. We are, in general, a rich country, but more and more people are using our food banks and being pushed into the marginalized segment. So, for a significant portion of the population, the reason why many parents were not reading to their kids was because they could not afford books.

The Scottish Book Trust focused their efforts on solving this second cause. Logically, the appeal was quite simple: *Will you make a donation to buy a book for a parent who cannot afford one to read to their child?* However, the easy assumption here was that the "maybes" – i.e. the target audience – were people who had empathy for the parent or the child and that the Scottish Book Trust should emphasize the direct connection with the plight of the parent or child in their fundraising communications.

To some extent, this assumption was true. But the actual target audience for the Scottish Book Trust, their "maybes," were book lovers. These were not donors who usually gave to children's charities; these were people in a unique segment of their own who loved books. So the direct connection the Scottish Book Trust was seeking to emphasize was not with the parent or child; it was with the book. The emotion was every bit as much about the book as it was about a parent or child living in poverty.

Once the Scottish Book Trust realized this, they took a step back and looked at where these unique donors' emotional connections to books came from. In all likelihood, it was from the donor's own life experience of being read to as a child or reading to their children. But the focal point was not the bonding exercise between parent and child; it was the visceral, memorable experience these donors had with the books themselves.

Our creative director, Dave Sturdy, looked at this data and came up with a brilliant insight. He said, "This is about missing books. We have to make these donors realize the richness of their emotional experience with these books. We have to get them to imagine what their life would be like, or how it would be different, if these books – and the wonder of discovering them for the first time – had not been available to them."

This manifested into a clear appeal: *What would you have missed out on if the books you love never existed? Because this is the reality for so many parents and children in Scotland.* It led to an exceptional series of creative treatments. One ad shows Pooh from *Winnie the Pooh* saying to Piglet, "I think we've been left on the shelf." Another focused on the *Tiger Who Came to Tea*, with copy that read:

The Tiger Who Didn't Come In
In Olivia's house, the tiger didn't come to tea . . . he wasn't invited.
Fewer children are being read to at home than ever before.
Will you buy a book to share with a child like Olivia?

(continued)

(continued)

Each of these creative briefs was accompanied by the classic illustrations that every person associates with these books and their characters. The creative treatment the trust ended up using is based on the *Gruffalo* series. In *The Gruffalo*, a mouse wanders through a forest and escapes a series of predators – a fox, an owl, and a snake – by telling them about a bigger, imaginary predator, the Gruffalo. It turns out the Gruffalo is real, and when the mouse encounters him, he has to use his wits to escape yet again. The Scottish Book Trust used this premise to create powerful, heart-rending copy:

To Isla, there really is no such thing as a Gruffalo.
Isla doesn't get read to at bedtime. Will you buy a book to share with her?

It was such a successful fundraising campaign that, in a small country, the Scottish Book Trust managed to raise tens of thousands of pounds in a very short period of time, just before Christmas. They used that money to buy many, many children's books that they then distributed, with some placed in food banks in the run-up to Christmas. Whenever someone went to a food bank to get a meal for their family for the holidays, they were offered a pile of books to give to their child as a Christmas present. It was a phenomenal fundraising campaign – one of the most focused I have seen. And it all started from clearly identifying and understanding their donors.

Key Takeaways

Human beings have a natural need to contribute to society, but there are several factors driving that need. Some people give to heal a wound in their life, others to find happiness and connection, still others to build self-esteem and create a life with meaning. Why a person gives, and what they need to give to, is shaped by their emotional histories, which in turn shapes their values.

To be a Great Fundraising Organization and meet the needs of your donors, you have to first identify your audience and discover what their needs are. Human beings are complex creatures, and a variety of factors intersect to create surprising results, so it takes hard work and focus to truly discover who your donor is and what they want. The first thing to remember is that your donor is not the same as the people who work in your organization: they don't have the same needs, wants, or emotional reactions.

Next, look for your "maybes." This is the audience whose emotional history aligns with your organization's but who haven't donated to you as yet because your communications haven't connected with them. Our data shows that the "maybe" segment of your market is where growth lies; they exist in the sweet spot where the "why" of your organization intersects with the "why" of your donor.

Lastly, once you have found your "maybes," you can use different models to better identify and understand their needs. There are many data models that do this provided by agencies and data analytics companies. We tend to prefer three models – the psychographic, biology, and identity models – but there is no right answer here or, indeed, one answer that works for all organizations. You must choose the one that suits you best.

(continued)

(continued)

Above all, look to identify a problem or need that aligns your organization internally but differentiates it externally. This takes hard work. Data helps, but it cannot give you the answers; that takes insight, analysis, and consistent simplification.

Lightbulb moments require persistence. But once you have that light, you can use it to illuminate the path forward.

Chapter 9

Meeting Donor Needs

Creating Great Fundraising Communications

In 2019, after 195 years of being one of the original Great Fundraising Organizations, the RNLI suffered a blip. Their fundraising revenue dropped off, and they began to lose their share of the legacy market, which was incredibly important to them. The long-term effects of this would have been dramatic for the organization, so they knew they had to fix it, and fix it immediately.

The problem, they realized, was that the call on the RNLI had changed. One hundred ninety-five years ago it was single minded; they launched lifeboats, primarily to commercial, fishing, or military vessels that were in trouble. The mission was to "preserve life from shipwreck." It was one simple calling, so it was easy to communicate the RNLI's activities.

But across the decades, the RNLI's work transformed. For one, the leisure use of water had increased, so a large percentage of their shouts now were for people closer to the coast, as opposed to large ships out at sea. Second, they had learned that prevention was better than cure, so they created a global mission to stop drowning through education. Then there were a thousand smaller projects they focused on: putting a lifeguard on a beach, for example, or ensuring a person of African origin had the right swim cap for their hair so they could learn to swim. It was more difficult to convey the complexity and variety of what they did with any precision.

In early 2019 we held a seminar to find their new ambition at IJmuiden, a port in Amsterdam, at the offices of their Dutch sister organization, KNRM. Our view from those offices was the Dutch rescue boats docked at port, which was a lovely reminder of what the RNLI stands for.

For a long time, we couldn't find any resolution to the RNLI's core problem: how should they educate people on the breadth of their work? We narrowed down a list of the main problems they were solving, at which point we were stuck. So we shifted gears. No more thinking in a logical, intellectual space. We moved to an emotional space, immersed ourselves in it, and then waited for the magic to pop.

After one and a half hours of sharing stories, it became obvious that while all the stories at the RNLI had a different beginning, they all had the same ending.

In 1824, the story was simple. A person, predominately a professional mariner, boarded a ship to go somewhere, the ship would get into trouble due to unforeseen weather conditions or equipment failure, and a lifeboat would come to save them.

In 2019, the story had a hundred different beginnings. The beginning could be a mother on a busy Bournemouth beach taking her eye off her child for a few seconds. It could be a father in Bangladesh who was too busy working so he could provide for his family to give his child swimming lessons. It could be a group of teenagers visiting Camber Sands who didn't understand the tides, a walker cut off by rising tides, a swimmer caught out by a rip current, or a crew member of a fishing trawler in Peterhead, Scotland, hitting an unexpected storm and having to be rescued at sea.

There were a hundred different beginnings, but the end of every story was the same. Somebody went into the water and came out again. Sometimes they came out alive. Sometimes they came out dead.

As long as there were still people coming out of the water dead, the RNLI needed more money to save more lives.

Silence in the room. Then Jayne George, the RNLI's excellent and newly appointed director of fundraising, said, "Surely it cannot be as simple as 'save everyone'?"

It was that simple, but it was not very emotional. We needed more punch for a new ambition. Máiréad, their in-house copy-writer, suggested a very simple change: a space between "every" and "one." This changed it from an abstract concept to the story of every individual.

To this day, the RNLI's new ambition is "To Save Every One." They launched it with what they called a "Perfect Storm" appeal in the United Kingdom and Ireland, which stated, *More people are using the water than ever before. Too many of them are still drowning. We don't have enough money to save every one – donate and help us.* That single appeal reversed their fundraising decline and began a period of unprecedented growth. "To Save Every One" became the creative brief for every fundraising communication: individual giving appeals, monthly giving, face-to-face or digital donations, major donor propositions and participation events such as Mayday, the appeal text used by hundreds of their volunteer branches across the United Kingdom.

All of this kicked off in October 2019. Six months later, the COVID-19 pandemic hit.

This could have been a disaster for the RNLI. Much of their fund-raising was done face to face, with volunteer teams across the United Kingdom generating regional revenue. This was now impossible thanks to the pandemic. But the refreshed focus created by their new ambition, as well as the change in their culture and the investment they had made in October to roll out the new ambition, meant that their other fundraising streams compensated for the drop in regional fundraising. They continued to grow.

Five years later, in 2024, the RNLI announced that their revenue was up by £58 million compared to 2019. This was on an annual basis, representing an income increase of 30% from an already high starting point, going against market trends in the United Kingdom and Ireland.

Royal National Lifeboat Institution

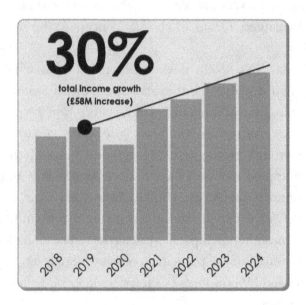

Figure 9.1 The Royal National Lifeboat Institution growth chart. *Source*: Revolutionise International Limited 2024.

Great fundraising communications start with a brilliant new ambition, which helps you find the right stories that can meet your donors' needs.

Meeting Donor Needs

Across Chapters 3 and 4, we looked at the key ingredients of a powerful new ambition and explained how it creates both alignment within your organization, as well as differentiation for your organization in the wider, competitive market. But how does this translate into the task of creating fundraising communications? How does it address what we have been talking about in Chapters 7 and 8: i.e. this emotional space that a nonprofit primarily exists in? In other words, what is the connection between the new ambition (which shapes your fundraising communications) and meeting your donors' needs (which is what your fundraising communications must achieve to generate revenue)?

The link lies in the details of building out your fundraising communications. A good way to think about it is via a hierarchy chart:

Figure 9.2 Building out your fundraising communications.
Source: Revolutionise International Limited 2024.

The new ambition is the big, long-term problem you are looking to solve, a goal that is mostly impossible. For the RNLI, it was "To Save Every One." Your new ambition can then be broken down into subsidiary problems that address the unique cases of your service users. So in the case of the RNLI, this would be the myriad different projects they were tackling in their modern form: teaching children to swim, training lifeguards, giving people equal access to the water by making sure they have the right gear, etc. Each of these subsidiary problems can be brought out by different stories, and each of these stories provides different proposed solutions (i.e. ways in which the donor can help). These, in turn, address the individual donor's needs that we talked about identifying in Chapter 8.

The key takeaway to keep in mind is that your new ambition is always grand, impossible, and singular, but the stories you tell about that new ambition can be varied, and these varied stories address unique donor needs. A nonprofit often has multiple donor bases, and our data shows that if we look at the same overarching problem but with different donors in mind, it can transform how we communicate with each donor to meet their needs.

Union Rescue Mission (URM) is a nonprofit battling homelessness in Los Angeles, United States. It has been around for a long time and is based right in the middle of Skid Row. During the pandemic, the homeless population was the worst hit, and URM saw a steep rise in the number of people arriving at their center. It prompted their CEO, Reverend Andy Bales, to seek to increase their fundraising income to improve capacity and operations.

When URM began to develop their new ambition, they found that they were tackling two different problems, each of which addressed the unique needs of a completely different set of donors.

The first was the direct problem of homelessness. In simplest terms, the solution to homelessness is a home. Similar to the RNLI, the beginning of a URM service user's story may differ – there may be many social, economic, and environmental factors that pushed them out onto the street – but the ending was always the same: someone was without a home. In the richest country in the world, it should be a basic human right to have somewhere to live.

This problem appealed to a certain kind of donor: people who considered philanthropy as divorced from religion and who donated from a human rights lens to solve problems. To target this donor, URM created a series of fundraising communications that told the truth about service users who found themselves homeless and at Skid Row, often with their families and children, through no fault of their own. The message was simply *Your donation will help someone find a home.*

The second problem was more hidden. Almost everyone living on Skid Row became addicted to something, be that alcohol, drugs, or glue. This meant that the first step when someone arrived at URM was often the fast and urgent treatment of this addiction because without overcoming it, the person was incapable of holding down an income or a home.

Now, ample research has shown that addiction is primarily a disease of stress and isolation. Connection with other people is the first step to curing addiction, and this was the work URM focused on: offering people who turned up at the Mission the love of, and connection with, others.

It is notoriously difficult to raise money to cure addiction compared to addressing homelessness. But URM had a second donor base: socially minded evangelical Christians. These donors wanted to share their money to help people overcome their troubles, but they also wanted to share their love. This was not to convert people to Christianity; it was a simple sense of connectedness with others that they wanted to share and that was integral to their giving. They did not want to give and go away. They wanted to be involved and share their compassion.

This meant URM had a donor base that wanted to give money and love, and they had service users walking through their doors who needed precisely those two elements. In order to meet these donors' needs, URM had to involve them in the addiction recovery program. The organization came up with a solution: each time someone arrived at the shelter, an alert was sent out to the donor base – preserving the anonymity of the service user, of course. The donors were then invited to a prayer meeting. As the meeting took place, the service user was made aware that other people were sending them their love and care right now. They were not alone, no matter how much they might believe they were. It was incredibly powerful.

This is what we mean when we say different donors need different stories, and those stories can describe subsidiary problems that, in turn, feed into the overarching problem or new ambition. URM created two completely different stories for their donor bases. One was a story about a family experiencing homelessness through no fault of their own. The other was about a person who had become addicted due to their homelessness through no fault of their own and who needed love to heal.

Good fundraising communications is about telling the right story to the right person. The shape of that story is guided by your new ambition, but the focus and detail of that story are designed to meet unique donor needs.

Exquisite Stories

Let us be in no doubt: at the heart of good fundraising is the ability to find and tell exquisite stories.

This is not as easy as it sounds. Often, gathering stories within an organization can be a challenge due to internal fears about telling these stories or the difficulty of contacting service users. Once you have these stories, it is also important to understand them at a core level so you can present them in a way that addresses your donors' needs.

So what are the elements of good storytelling in the field of fundraising? Our data shows that powerful stories have both an itch and a scratch, which means the donor must feel like there is an injustice or problem that must be corrected (itch) and that they have the power to correct it (scratch). It must also be a simple truth well-told, which we discussed in Chapter 7.

Research tells us that the story of one person, animal, or family is the most effective in fundraising communications. Nineteen times out of 20, the single story outperforms everything else. Evidence also proves that longer stories – or rather, stories that are as long as they need to be – are the most effective in bringing in donations. This might seem counterintuitive, but we have been able to do split tests across a huge volume, and the data is conclusive: independent of media, long stories are what connect with donors.

But the most essential DNA of an exquisite story in fundraising, the amino acid that builds everything else, is what we call the "sliding door" story.

We named it the sliding door story in tribute to the Gwyneth Paltrow movie called *Sliding Doors*. At the opening of that movie, Paltrow is running to catch a train before the doors close. At that moment, the movie splits. In one reality, she makes it onto the train, and in another reality, the doors slide shut in front of her. The movie then follows both reality streams, showing how one moment in time can drastically alter the course of a person's life.

In the fundraising sliding door story, you start by telling a story of a person or animal from left to right – from the very beginning, in a linear manner. Then there is a moment where something happens and everything changes. This moment could be a natural disaster. It could be the diagnosis of a disease or a moment of abandonment. It is a life-altering event.

At this point, the story splits. From here, it can have only two outcomes. Either it has a good ending or a bad ending. The difference between those two endings is a donation that someone is about to give your nonprofit.

Figure 9.3   Sliding door story.
Source: Revolutionise International Limited 2024.

The sliding door story invites donors to turn someone's bad ending into a good one. Communicating this clearly with appropriate connection, empathy, agency, and dignity is the skill of the fundraising communicator. Everything else is a multiple of this insight.

Here is the key, though: most people think it is the good endings that get you the money, but it is not. It is the bad ending. You may have a thousand stories with good endings that show how excellent your nonprofit is at saving lives, but from a fundraising perspective, these are a thousand reasons why you do not need more money. The reason you need more money is the story with a bad ending. *That* is the person your nonprofit could not reach at the current capacity, and that is why you need donations – to save others like them.

Tell the story with a bad ending. I offered this insight to a room of 200 people in Johannesburg, South Africa, and a woman near the front let out a long moan. It was part Eureka moment, part frustration, and part relief. When I spoke to her after the seminar, she said, "Why was this not the first thing we were taught in our fundraising education? For 15 years, I've been hammering on about stories with a good ending, when a bad ending would have made the difference."

My own discovery of the sliding door story was surprising. Back in 2008, when I was a volunteer on the board of a mental health charity, I was invited to do a presentation at the House of Commons. I did what we all do in these situations: I made a detailed and factual PowerPoint about the organization and their success statistics. It was our chief psychiatrist who talked me out of it.

"Alan, this is rubbish," he said. "Everyone does this. I know the story of why you are on the board. Tell that story instead."

So I did. It was a story about me and my best friend. She and I had been very close, but we gradually lost touch when I moved to the other side of the country. She fell on hard times, particularly with horrific bullying in the workplace. She found herself with terrible mental health and absolutely no one to talk to. She hung herself.

At the time of the presentation, I was going through my own mental health crisis. The difference between me and my friend was I had two people who would not give up on speaking to me. They would not let me isolate. They would call, they would bang on my door, they would force me out for walks. The only reason I was standing at the House of Commons to tell this story and my once best friend was dead was I had two people to speak to and she had nobody.

This was the solution my charity provided to people with depression and why I was volunteering my time. We asked people to give money so that the next person in a mental health crisis would pick up the telephone instead of a bottle of pills.

This was my first ever sliding door story, and I found it was such a powerful way to communicate what a nonprofit hopes to achieve and why. Since then, I have watched the impact of a sliding door story play out again and again at an organizational level, not just in terms of meeting donor needs but also for aligning nonprofit culture.

Consider the RNLI in that October of 2019. They had just come up with their new ambition, "To Save Every One," and they were in the process of aligning their communications with that ambition. For credibility reasons, the RNLI had been broadcasting their success statistics. They were telling donors how good their response times were, how courageous their crew was, how many lives they saved. In other words, they were broadcasting the solution – the many good endings.

This made their volunteer crew uncomfortable. These were humble, mission-driven people, and they were being asked to share how amazing they were on social media. It did not sit well with their personalities.

So when the RNLI were thinking through the new communications for "To Save Every One," we came up with a different approach. We decided that RNLI did not need money because they saved so many lives but because there were so many lives they could not save. We asked their volunteer crew, "Do you have stories of the ones you couldn't save?"

The response was overwhelming. Not only did practically every crew member have a story about someone they could not save, but they were eager to tell it. They wanted to share because it spoke to a fear they grappled with every day: going out on rescue and leaving someone behind or not being able to find someone at sea.

Those stories were transformational. I have never seen anything better for organizational enlightenment. These anecdotes were being told straight from the horse's mouth, by people who took their boats out into storms and battled with the greatest dangers to save lives. Then they lived with the pain and regret for those they couldn't save.

The RNLI's new fundraising communications came directly from the crew. They were stories about the people they had lost: "Last week we saved five lives. The only two I can think about are the ones we couldn't save." It had an immediate, emotional impact.

In every organization we have worked with, there are people who want to tell their story, either because it is of benefit to them or because it benefits them to help others by telling their story. Look for these people. These stories are always there if you are prepared to put in the effort and seek with integrity. Storytelling can be an empowering tool that lets people speak their truth and that forges a human connection between service user, volunteer, and donor.

Creating Great Fundraising Communications

So let's pull back and put together everything we have explored about the new ambition, donor needs, and good storytelling. How do we implement these elements to create great fundraising communications?

There are, of course, many methodologies to shaping fundraising communications, but our research is emphatic that there are four elements, executed in a particular order, that will give your organization internal alignment and external differentiation:

1. New ambition
2. Exquisite but long stories
3. Proposed solution
4. Creative treatment

You start with the new ambition because that becomes the focal point that aligns your organization toward a long-term goal and defines your fundraising communications. You then look for and gather exquisite stories. These are simple truths well-told, diversified for your organization's many donor bases and needs. The stories should be long and should communicate both an itch and a scratch. The structure of the sliding door story can be incredibly powerful, because it shows your donor how they can change someone's bad ending into a good one.

The direct proposed solution then clarifies that feeling by explaining *how* the donor can solve the problem by donating. There are two types of proposed solutions. The first is where a nonprofit promises that the donated money will be earmarked for solving a particular problem. This is usually reserved for very big gifts. The second type of proposed solution is when a nonprofit gives an example of the type of problem the donor's gift can solve so that the donor knows what they are contributing toward.

A key insight for framing your proposed solution is that fundraising ultimately solves one of two problems: death or loneliness. If you can figure out how your organization is solving either death or loneliness (or some combination of them), then you will have come a long way toward framing a tangible proposed solution.

An excellent example of this is Solar Aid, an international NGO that creates sustainable markets for solar lighting in sub-Saharan Africa via philanthropy. Most of their work is at the top level, but it is too sophisticated, long-term, and complex to attract new donors. To create effective fundraising, they needed to articulate an immediate problem the donor could solve.

Finding that problem was tricky. Solar lighting can solve many issues: climate change, economic fragility, cost of power across sub-Saharan Africa. But, using the insight about death and loneliness, Solar Aid asked themselves, *How does solar power, at the most basic human level, solve death or loneliness?*

It led to an uncomfortable truth. There are parts of the world in which darkness plus poverty equals death. A simple solar light could disrupt that equation. Solar Aid created a stunning series of creatives that showed donors how the proposed solution (*donate so we can buy solar lights*) would create tangible change. The proposed solution was simple but immensely powerful.

For example, they described how a woman's baby died when a candle set a mosquito net on fire. If that woman had solar light, her baby would still be alive. Or they talked about a grandmother who came home at night in the pitch black and never saw the snake hiding in her bed. If she had a solar light, she could have escaped. Each fundraising communication had the same message: "Darkness is deadly. Give a solar light, save a life."

Moreover, Solar Aid's proposed solution could be scaled. You could fund one solar light for a household, or you could buy a solar light system for a hospital or an orphanage. In each case, big or small, you saved lives.

Lastly, there is the creative treatment. The mistake organizations make is they start with the creative treatment and then work backward, along the four points, because they assume the only thing that matters is grabbing attention. Attention is important, but it is not what gets you the money. Having a differentiated, better product that addresses your donors' needs is how you get people to donate. You do this by starting with the new ambition and working down the list.

But once you have your new ambition, have found your stories, and have decided your proposed solution, how do you execute a creative treatment that gets people's attention? The key question is *why* do you want people's attention? It is not to tell them how good or successful your nonprofit is. It is to get them to read the story that outlines the problem and your proposed solution. That's it. You get people's attention so that they listen to the work you have done to differentiate your organization because it is this differentiation that brings in donations.

Our data here is conclusive: the best way to get someone's attention is to tell them a detail of the story that makes them want to hear the rest of it. Find that detail and blow it up into your headline.

Headlines do not make money, nor do photographs. But headlines and photographs together can get people to pay attention long enough to hear the rest of the story and connect with what the nonprofit is offering.

Where Does Brand Fit In?

Since our original research on the Great Fundraising Organizations, there have been many questions about branding and fundraising. A nonprofit's brand is, of course, their identity and their credibility as an organization. How should fundraising communications interact with branding?

To find out, we commissioned one of the first-ever studies on branding, fundraising, and their effect on each other. We discovered that the key to understanding the relationship circles back to the foundation we discussed in Chapter 1: two businesses, one mission. Each business has a different communications channel, as we talked about in Chapter 3: the business focused on the donor has "fundraising communications," while the business focused on the service user has "theory of change." Both of these communication channels meet at the level of branding.

The mistake that many organizations make is believing that good branding requires a similar message across both businesses of the charity. It does not. Branding provides consistency and personality but not integration. This means your brand decides the recognizability of your content and a consistent tone of voice, style, and visual identity across your organization, but it does not seek to integrate the message of your two businesses into one. These must be separate: fundraising communications should brand the problem correctly (to inspire donations), while theory of change must correctly brand the solution (to build credibility).

The Great Fundraising Organizations always ask themselves, *What is our brand for?* It is a good question to think about instead of considering brand as independent of organizational purpose. When organizations suffer a backslide or halt in their fundraising growth, they often look to rebranding as a solution. Prior to Jayne's and our intervention, this is what some were suggesting the RNLI needed to do in 2019. They were considering rebranding from "Save lives at sea" to "Save lives together" so as to reflect the breadth of their work.

Once we got involved, we convinced them otherwise. "Save lives together" could be any charity in the world. "Save lives at sea" could only be the RNLI. They were about to throw away 195 years' worth of heritage and differentiation because it looked like the simple solution: to describe everything they do rather than describe the problem they solve.

Another great example of how this thinking created a breakthrough is UNICEF. We were commissioned by their head office in Geneva to provide leadership education and cocreation sprints for their numerous country offices and national committees. Bear in mind that the UNICEF brand is nonnegotiable across all their countries. This is with very good reason: they have an influencing and negotiating mandate at a governmental level across the globe, which means that their brand "For every child" must be recognizable so as to present their credibility without compromise. In other words, the promise UNICEF makes – i.e. "For every child" – has to be the same everywhere.

However, the *problem* that fundraising is designed to solve can differ dramatically from country to country. This means that the same set of fundraising communications may work in one place but not in another – and the many country offices of UNICEF had to meet this challenge head on. Yes, the UNICEF brand had to stay the same, but each fundraising department had to rework their fundraising communications to capture the problem they were uniquely trying to solve with that brand.

For example, in Norway, all the money raised was used for projects in other countries or to increase UNICEF's influence with governments and populations. The problem they were trying to solve, therefore, was: *We know the solutions, but we need more money because there are children and people we cannot yet reach in time.* The country's new ambition was therefore to help the global UNICEF organization to reach more children until, one day, they managed "To reach every child in time." It was a sophisticated and simple reworking.

The reworking was more complex in Argentina. UNICEF in Argentina spends much of its fundraising revenue in Argentina itself. How then were they to craft fundraising communications that spoke directly to their parent organization's brand? It turned out that the problem they were trying to solve was *children are in danger due to recurrent economic crises that increase levels of child poverty.* It was an intergenerational problem. Their new ambition became "Be the generation that gets our children out of danger," which, of course, was in clear dialogue with UNICEF's global brand of "for every child." This united the fundraising and advocacy campaigns, and the Argentinian office launched an integrated campaign called "Guardavidas De La Infancia," which means "Lifeguards of the Children." Their team did the creative execution internally, and it is one of the best treatments and launches I have ever seen. Local problem, global brand.

This is why it matters to ask *what is our brand for?* Even if a brand must stay constant across geographies, as in the case of UNICEF, asking what your brand is for helps you articulate the unique problems you are tackling and craft a new ambition that addresses these problems. In other words, the brand is not your purpose – the brand is *for* your purpose. There may be cases where rebranding is the correct solution to kickstart fundraising growth, as it was for CHAS in Chapter 3. If you keep coming back to that question, it will help you tell the difference. As long as rebranding is for a purpose and not *the* purpose, you are on the right path.

Illustration: Institute for Justice and Reconciliation, South Africa

At the end of the apartheid government in South Africa, Nelson Mandela established the Truth and Reconciliation Commission (TRC), with Desmond Tutu as head, to examine the human rights violations that took place during apartheid and to heal a broken country. After the TRC dissolved, the Institute for Justice and Reconciliation (IJR) was set up as a nonprofit to further TRC's work.

For many years, IJR made slow and steady progress. Then, in the 2010s, they suffered a backslide. Due to a number of factors, it seemed that a lot of their good work was being undone. IJR realized they needed to reboot and refocus before moving forward.

When IJR reevaluated their organization, they found that their work had expanded since their establishment. Similar to the RNLI, they now found themselves with multiple beginnings to their stories.

One story, for example, was of a child in the apartheid era, watching his father retrieve a beach ball that had rolled from the "Blacks-only" area of the bus to the front, the "Whites-only" area. He watched as white men beat the shit out of his father.

Another story was of a mother writing to her son, who had to leave South Africa for New Zealand because of the threats from thugs who were unhappy with how progressive he was. She wrote, "I am so sorry you had to leave our beautiful country just because you didn't fit. But I am so proud of you for not fitting."

A third story was of a lesbian Black woman in Soweto who was flung into jail because the cops didn't like her short hair. "You look like a boy," they told her, "so you can go into the men's cell." She was raped by 12 men in that cell and died of her injuries.

(continued)

Meeting Donor Needs

(continued)

IJR's stories were vast and varied, but they added up to the same problem: deep divisions across multiple axes in modern South Africa. It was a similar issue to what they faced in the 1980s and 1990s, except now IJR identified more divisions than they would have anticipated at the end of apartheid: economic, racial, cultural, sexuality, tribal, and linguistic divisions. IJR articulated this problem as "Divided we fall." If South Africa could not find a way to heal as a nation, they would not survive.

The solution was to use nation-building to unite people over time. The divisions were so varied, however, that it was clear it would take an enormous timespan to achieve reconciliation. I remember Stanley Henkeman, their CEO, asking a room full of IJR colleagues: "Who believes we will solve this problem in our lifetime?"

No one put up their hand.

"Who believes our children will solve this problem?"

No one raised their hands.

"Who believes our grandchild will solve it?"

There was a pause, and then a woman at the back of the room raised her hand. She said, "I don't think our grandchildren will solve it. But I also never thought we would end the apartheid regime, so I am going to take a leap of faith."

One person in a room full of committed, passionate people believed that the task in front of them was possible to achieve in their grandchild's lifetime – and her belief was a leap of faith. It was clear the problem they were tackling was monumental. But it was also clear that they would work tirelessly until they solved it. Stan said, "In my mind, this is now a 100-year intergenerational campaign."

IJR decided to kick off the campaign in 2019, which was the centenary of Mandela's birth. To everyone sitting in that room, the dates held special significance. A hundred years since Mandela's birth meant Mandela had only taken South Africa halfway. The country needed another 100 years, and another incredible effort, to go the whole distance.

IJR launched in 2019 with the new ambition "A 100-year dream of a united South Africa."

I have many stories of organizations that have executed fundraising communications to an impeccable degree at a granular level. But this book is about big-picture, broader thinking and the philosophy that powers the Great Fundraising Organizations. IJR is a brilliant case study of how the new ambition embodies a unifying problem that is made up of many subsidiary problems. If chosen correctly, a new ambition can align your organization internally and differentiate it externally while shaping the stories that drive donor connection.

Key Takeaways

Great fundraising communications are composed of four elements, executed in order: the new ambition, exquisite storytelling, the proposed solution, and the creative treatment.

Crafting great fundraising communications begins with a new ambition: it is the vision and impossible problem you are trying to solve that captures the subsidiary problems of your organization. Each subsidiary problem can yield its own story that, in

(continued)

Meeting Donor Needs

(continued)

turn, can speak to the different donor bases of your charity and meet their needs. This is why the new ambition should form the creative brief for every fundraising communication.

At the core of good fundraising is exquisite storytelling. The sliding door story can be powerful in showing your donor how their gift can change a bad ending into a good one. Remember to not focus only on the good endings; it is the bad ending that drives fundraising growth because it shows your donor why you need more money. Also remember that different donors need different stories to meet their needs.

The proposed solution explains to your donor how they can solve your problem by donating – in other words, how their money can help you make the world a better place. Bear in mind that fundraising solves one of two problems: death or loneliness. If you can connect your proposed solution to one of these two elements (and there is always a way), you will have crafted a powerful appeal.

Last but not least, design your creative treatment to get attention – but not for attention's sake. Shape your creative treatment so that people will listen to your story and your proposed solution. Ultimately, fundraising communications is not just about grabbing people's attention. It means having a better offer from the rest of your competition and then getting people's attention.

Chapter 10

Financial Leadership

Readers might be curious as to why financial leadership is in Part II of this book, under "emotional excellence." In my experience, there is very little in this world that is more emotional than money. Perhaps food and love but not much else.

People get intensely emotional about money, particularly about risk. Investing can be scary, often paralyzing to comprehend, forget to implement. Many people seek to overcome that fear by looking for certainty in numbers and returns. But of course, as we saw in Chapter 2, the key differentiator between a leader and a manager is the ability to live with uncertainty and to work from a more abstract, unformed space.

In our masterclasses, we project a questionnaire onto a screen and ask delegates to score their organizational capacity based on two different financial measures. The column on the left looks at income and expenses account, balance sheet, cash flows, and lifetime value measurement. The column on the right focuses on test planning, investment modeling, forecasting and then budgeting KPIs, and so on. The scoring is from 1 to 5, with 1 being "awful" and 5 "good." Then we ask the delegates to add up each column for the total figure for the two different strands.

When everyone has finished the task, I ask the room, "Raise your hand if your score on the left column is higher than the score on the right." On every single occasion, at least 80% raise their hands.

How front foot are you on the following?
(1 = awful   5 = great)

Topic	Score
Income and expense account	
Balance sheet	
Including fund allocations	
Cash-flow analysis	
Life-time value measurement	
Cost per acquisition analysis	
Reporting results	

Topic	Score
Investment modeling	
Test planning	
Forecasting	
Budgeting, including if/then scenarios	
Predictive KPIs	
Cost/profit center analysis	
Reporting learnings	

Figure 10.1 How front foot are you on the following?
Source: Revolutionise International Limited 2024.

Occasionally, it is 100% of the room. More often than not, the difference between the two scores is significant.

The reason is simple. The items in the left column are a legal mandate for nonprofits, so they are exceptional at executing them. But no charity is mandated to complete the tasks on the right column, which means these items often fall by the wayside.

But here is the problem. Everything in the left column is about accounting for the past, while everything in the right column is about predicting and modeling the future. We have done this enough times now to have significant data to say that the fundraising sector as a whole is exceptional at fulfilling its legal mandate, but it is significantly underequipped, under-tooled, and under-resourced, in the main, regarding its ability to model and predict finances into the future.

Why is this a problem? Because being able to predict finances into the future is what allows you to make financial decisions now. It is impossible to decide how much investment you need to manage and balance your portfolio and to move money to where opportunities are the greatest if you do not know what the potential returns are. Without that data, you are simply guessing.

Guessing is scary. Guessing is why organizations would rather not invest in fundraising growth – because they cannot understand, recognize, and measure the upside. As we saw in Chapter 5, *not* investing can be disastrous: you need to be able to make middle- to long-term investments to trigger, maintain, and accelerate fundraising growth.

The right column is not a "nice to have." It is essential. Modeling potential returns overcomes emotional barriers; it allows leadership to make investment decisions in the present in a less fearful manner, with clearer analysis, helping you trigger the Red Dot. Let's look at how.

Understand Lifetime Value and Growth

A question that often comes up when we discuss long-term thinking and future-proofing an organization is "What is considered long term?" This can often fly off into a detailed discussion about "lifetime value."

Simply put, the "lifetime value" of a donor is how much money the nonprofit believes a donor will give over their lifetime. Organizations can get actuarial about this and focus on data and statistics to help calculate this figure. Post-life gifts (i.e. legacy gifts) are often the biggest, and more data can help a charity get more specific about the lifetime value of a donor cohort.

The danger here is that these calculations can get extremely academic, and organizations can get bogged down in the data. We have found that, as opposed to lifetime value, it is more useful to consider one's decision-making horizon. So, look at your 5-, 7- or 10-year time period – the cycle of a new ambition and a Red Dot – and then calculate what an investment now will get you across this decision-making horizon.

This means that the Great Fundraising Organizations have additional metrics for the fundraising and finance departments that focus on that right hand–side column discussed earlier, metrics that help leadership make long-term investment decisions.

In organizations that struggle, the metrics that are recorded and analyzed are the ones that do not focus on growth. These metrics focus on a short-term view, which, as we touched upon in Part I, means the fundraising department is usually asked for three deliverables:

- Cash flow in the short-term to plug a gap so that the one-year statutory accounts look good
- Any spend within the financial year must produce a return within that financial year
- All the money raised must go into the unrestricted fund

There is no doubt that achieving a return within a financial year and having that return unrestricted makes the job of managing a nonprofit easier. But it never leads to the kind of growth that all charities want to achieve: growth that takes them closer to fulfilling their purpose. This is a classic case of where, if you want to accelerate toward your purpose, "easy" is not the same as "good."

Great Fundraising Organizations look at additional metrics when measuring financial and fundraising success, and these metrics focus on the future. The top-level metric used to drive growth is measuring the lifetime value of a donor and dividing that by the cost of getting that donor:

$$\text{Lifetime value (LTV)}/\text{Cost per acquisition (CPA)} =$$
$$\text{Return on investment (ROI)}$$

The term "ROI" is often misused in fundraising organizations to mean the short-term profit of an appeal, campaign, or program. The real ROI is measuring how much someone will give an organization for the rest of their life and dividing that by how much it costs to get them to make their first donation. Note that you should net out lifetime value because there is a cost of servicing donors across their lifetime to keep them with the organization.

In short, the long-term growth of an organization is driven by a pyramid of metrics that all line up to maximize this formula: LTV/CPA. The best way to decide these metrics is to start with this formula and then work out a set of predictive key performance indicators that tell you if you are maximizing LTV/CPA.

Anyone who has ever run a business will know that profit and growth are not the same thing. Fundraising profit is made in short-term detail and down in the weeds; it is those hundred items improving by 1% compounding. But *growth* is driven by the big picture, and that can only be shaped by long-term planning and thinking.

Organizations that are sophisticated at investment will be able to take the net lifetime value of a donor and give it a capital value based on what they consider to be an acceptable ROI. This is much like valuing a business in the private sector. Capital value can give them an index that is similar to a stock market index.

We have a client who has achieved this. They have an algorithm that scans their database and gives them a single number that represents the value of their database on that day. This is obviously not a real capital asset that a nonprofit can borrow or leverage against, but it has been remarkably inspiring for their fundraising team because it compounds the effect of every detail they carry out today to show the long-term effect. This means the team can see the future capital value of their efforts immediately.

By no means are we advocating that all organizations do this. Our client is extremely sophisticated with technology, and it is a tool that works well within their organizational context; it is not for everyone. But it is worth highlighting because the key metric here is the growth of the program rather than the profit.

Test to Make Ideas Work

Our action dataset threw up a very interesting insight, which is that Great Fundraising Organizations have a different approach to testing than other nonprofits. In the organizations that struggle, testing was a way to see if an idea works or not. But for the Great Fundraising Organizations, testing was a way to *make* something work.

The first approach is the classic one. Sometimes, when an organization comes up with a new perspective or idea, they will say, "Let's test it." They create half a dozen Facebook ads, bang them out for a week, and when these ads don't get a great response, the organization decides the idea doesn't work for them. We've seen many organizations operate with this mindset, often canning a program based on a single test.

The Great Fundraising Organizations use the concept of testing across their portfolio with a determination to learn more about their ideas and to iterate them until they become profitable. These organizations are not testing with the thought process of *if we invest a small amount on Monday, what do we have back by Friday?* Instead, they have a rigorous model, they feed their test results into that model, and they are able to determine what kind of returns that test will get in the long-term, particularly over lifetime value.

Why are modeling and predictive data so important? Because every fundraising director will, at some point, have to convince people who are not fundraisers or investors to support their plans. If these people can only see data for the short-term, they will consider the money you are requesting as a cost, not an investment, and decide it is money wasted. But, as we have seen across the course of this book, it *is* an investment. Think of FARM Africa, which spent a modest amount of money on legacy fundraising and reaped millions over the next 25 years. Any leader looking at the 25-year data would authorize that modest investment in a heartbeat; they would be foolish not to. This is the importance of predictive data: it gets leadership buy-in and aligns your nonprofit.

So how do Great Fundraising Organizations model and test to make an idea work? Here is an anonymous example of an organization executing a direct-response television campaign. They ran four stages of tests.

Test 1: Will Anyone Give to Us?

The first test was to discover if there was any market for their idea. To minimize risk, they spent a relatively small amount of money creating a basic TV ad to recruit monthly donations. They then ran that ad across a few slots on channels (chosen based on gut feelings of what would work).

Their success criterion was simple. They already had the data on how much money an average monthly donor gave to their organization across a 5- to 10-year period. Thus, based on the number of signups from the ad, they could produce a model that essentially said, "We spent x amount on the advertising campaign, and in five to ten years, we will get y amount back." Their aim was to break even in 2 years.

This first test had both positive and negative results. The positive was that people did sign up for monthly donations. The negative was that not enough people signed up to create enough value to make those advertising slots viable.

At this point, most organizations would deem the test a failure and conclude that TV didn't work for them. But this organization moved on to Test 2.

Test 2: Improve Cost per Acquisition

The organization asked themselves, *How do we get more donors per dollar we spend?* They ran a three-by-three test matrix, which means they tested three different media slots against three different proposed solutions to the donor.

This had a positive result in that the ROI dramatically improved but not to the point that they were happy with it as yet. At this stage, the breakeven period was about two and half years, and the fundraising team wanted to improve on this before asking the board for a larger investment budget.

Test 3: Look at All the Details

So they moved on to Test 3, which had a much bigger testing budget because Test 2 had been partially successful. Here, they were looking at how the 1 percent improvement of a hundred little details could make a difference. They examined different response mechanisms, different telephone numbers, different web copy, different voiceovers, and different TV channels and media slots. Their metric was a large, multidimensional matrix, and they were driving every detail to discover the sweet spot.

At this point, they hit their success criterion: they were now breaking even in under two years.

Test 4: How Do You Maximize Lifetime Value?

The fourth test took the success of the third test to the next level. So far, the organization had only looked at optimizing cost per acquisition. At stage four, they asked, *How do you maximize return or lifetime value?* They added the compound growth effect into the projections and began testing for the active program *after* someone had signed up, as opposed to the communications that got someone to sign up. In other words, they focused on donor development and on testing the third, fourth, or fifth communication with the donor after they had signed up to learn how to meet their needs better and increase lifetime value.

Once this test finished, the breakeven for the program was down to a little over a year. More importantly, the figure for the five-year period had compounded to a significant value. For this case study, it was a return of approximately 8:1. This was the point at which the fundraising team went to the board and asked for significant investment using this predictive data as proof of the viability of their ask.

These are the four stages of testing to make something work. A helpful way to remember them is:

1. Will anyone give to us?
2. Improve CPA
3. Optimize CPA
4. Add donor development

For some organizations, there is a bigger bonus on top of this: a stage five, where they add their legacy model to see the predicted value of an investment across a donor's lifetime and beyond.

Be Proactive

As director of fundraising, it is critical that you be *proactive* in developing the financial ability and decision-making capacity of your senior leadership team. It is, of course, the responsibility of the board and the director of finance to maintain financial control of a nonprofit; this is legally mandated, ethical, and best practice. But as the director of fundraising, you do have the power to steer your organization toward a more future-oriented financial approach through focused upward and sideways leadership.

The key group that drives fundraising investment in an organization is the board, the CEO, the finance director, and the fundraising director. Great fundraising leaders are active in developing the financial ability and decision-making of these stakeholders by providing the data, education, training, and confidence required for the senior leadership to adopt a future-oriented approach. I cannot emphasize this enough: great fundraising leaders are proactive not only about improving capacity to make leadership decisions but also about providing the *data* that the leadership needs to make these decisions and be reassured as the nonprofit tests and invests.

There are two tools that are extremely effective here. The first is predictive key performance indicators (KPIs), which are KPIs that look forward, not back. Ask yourself what KPIs can you produce that showcase not only how well you have done in the past but how well you will do in the future. These will become the pyramid of metrics we spoke about in the section "Understand Lifetime Value and Growth," which led up to the formula of LTV divided by CPA.

The second tool is scenario-based budgeting. Scenario-based budgeting is when you ask the board and senior leadership team for a significant investment but make that investment contingent on your short-term test results hitting a predecided success criterion (i.e. the scenario). A good example of this would be the case study we unpacked in the section "Test to Make Ideas Work" regarding the direct-response television campaign. The success criterion for those series of tests was to break even in under two years, after which the fundraising team could go back to the board and request further investment. Once they hit that success criterion, it was easier for the board to sign off on the investment because it was easier for the senior leadership team to assess and trust the idea.

Scenario-based budgeting is also an excellent way to create pace in an organization. Instead of running a test and then, if it is successful, waiting another 12 months for the budget cycle to complete and the new year's money to be available, fundraising directors can go to the board and say, "Set aside the investment money now and give us a test budget. If our tests hit a pre-agreed success criteria, allow us to automatically roll out."

Get on the Front Foot

A large part of being a great fundraising leader is managing the board and senior leadership to clear the path toward becoming a Great Fundraising Organization. Here are a few tips on how to help the senior leadership team more effectively support you when it comes to financial freedom.

Train Them on the Financials

The senior leadership and the board must be trained on fundraising financials. As we saw in Chapter 1, you cannot expect people to make decisions on investment unless they understand the returns and the benefits of that investment. Across our dataset, we discovered that alignment means the whole organization – or at least down its hierarchy as far as middle management – must have a minimum of a broad understanding of fundraising investment and how it works.

Change How You Report Progress and Learnings

In Chapter 2, we mentioned that the Trifecta is a leadership issue, which means it often exists in a space of uncertainty. So where do trust and confidence come from in the absence of certainty?

It comes from the board and senior leadership's trust in you as the director of fundraising and in your fundraising team's ability to learn and adapt to meet pre-agreed metrics. Therefore, as fundraising director, it is vital that you build up a track record of showing that you can make projections and deliver on them, as well as showcase how you are improving every week, month, and quarter through the program. This means meeting projections and presenting your learnings to the senior leadership team. What has been learned in the last quarter? How have you improved? What were the results of your testing? How has your capacity been built?

I have just met with my bank manager about a substantial investment in a hotel business that we own. Normally, you present three years of financials for this kind of loan, but we couldn't do that since, like most hotels across the world, our business was significantly damaged by the COVID-19 pandemic. So 12 months ago, we told the bank that we could not provide financials for the past three to five years but that we were confident our business was now back to its best and, for several reasons, had grown. Based on this, the bank and our organization reached an agreement. We would provide a set of projections for the following 12 months and if we met those projections, we would be eligible for a loan. A year has now passed, we have met our projections, and my bank manager just told me we are eligible for the loan.

This anecdote shows that trust can be built using forward-facing metrics. It is the same scenario as between a board and a fundraising team: the bank was willing to invest in an organization's ability to create predictions and then learn how to meet them.

Help the Senior Leadership Team Manage Risk

If you are embarking on a growth program, it is helpful to pre-agree on the points at which the board and senior leadership can review your progress. That way, rather than worrying every day, they know they will receive a report every quarter that lets them manage their risk on a slightly short-term basis. Moreover, work with scenarios; include an A, B, and C scenario so that the board and senior leadership are easily able to identify the line you are following and what growth projections look like.

Lastly, work with models and turn them into live forecasts as results come in. This means that as the long-term forecasts change, the leadership can see the change in their investment.

Be Financially Astute

To become a director of fundraising, you, of course, have to be financially astute. What we have observed from our dataset, however, is that many professional or career fundraisers who have risen through the ranks are financially astute when it comes to managing the income and expenses account but have received far less education in managing the balance sheet. This is particularly true for changes in the balance sheet over time.

To get on the front foot and effectively manage investment, you need broader expertise in both the income and expenditure sheet and the balance sheet. Thus, a dedicated tip to managing the senior leadership team and handling investment is to be as good at the balance sheet as you are at the income and expenditure sheet.

Illustration: Norges Blindeforbund, Norway

Approximately 35 years ago, Leif Wien Jensen took the job as director of fundraising at Norges Blindeforbund, a nonprofit for the blind and partially sighted in Norway. At the time, there were practically no fundraising organizations in Norway. The only few were large international organizations that were managing fundraising externally.

Leif decided to make it his life's work to turn Norges Blindeforbund into a Great Fundraising Organization. He traveled all over the world to attend conferences that could help him do this because there were no sources in Norway for him to turn to. Gradually, over these 35 years, he transformed Norges Blindeforbund into one of the best fundraising organizations I know. They do incredible work. There was no agency support for them at the time Leif started, so Leif built an in-house agency for both telephone and direct mail, as well as advertising work. There is no doubt he helped make Norges Blindeforbund a self-created Great Fundraising Organization.

A couple of years ago, we invited Leif to present at an annual skill share we host at our Loch Ness center, where successful organizations share insights with each other. Each speaker usually gives a 20-minute presentation followed by a 40-minute discussion.

When Leif turned up to Loch Ness for his presentation, he was a little nervous – which, if you know Leif, is unusual. I found him sitting at the front of our Loch Ness Center, staring out into Loch Ness. I joined him.

"I'm about to present something I have dreamed about for a long time," Leif told me, "and I'm just hopeful I'll get a good reaction to it."

Presentations at the skill share usually focus on inspiring stories, powerful and emotional communications, and brand work. Leif, however, did something surprising. He presented data instead.

For 35 years, Leif had been collecting data on Norges Blindeforbund – on their journey to becoming a Great Fundraising Organization, growing from a revenue of practically zero to millions of Norwegian Kroner. He knew this dataset intimately because he had stuck around for all of those 35 years to help build the organization to where they were now.

But Leif didn't just present the existing data. He presented the model he and his team had built to predict income and scenarios long, long into the future. It was an extremely sophisticated model, with a greater than 99% degree of certainty. It showed the board of Norges Blindeforbund exactly what they needed to do now to secure the future of the organization and grow for the next 40–50 years. The level of precision was mind-boggling. To say we were blown away is an understatement.

Predicting results is one thing, but the model was also used to enhance them. Leif knows all about meeting donor needs, and he worked with a professor from Copenhagen Business School to interrogate his model and data and identify exact moments in the donor journey where they should focus to improve satisfaction and income.

What struck me was how purpose driven a fundraiser had to be to not only stay in an organization for 35 years but then to future-proof it for the next fifty. Through this model, Leif ensured that everything he had learned would be embedded, in data, so that the quality of the program and its growth would continue long after his retirement.

Leif is not retired now, and he's unlikely to do so in the near future. But 50 years from now, Leif will not be around, and yet he

(continued)

(continued)

was determined that his 35 years of learning would not be lost. His drive and passion would ensure, through one of the most incredible pieces of forward-looking data I have seen, that Norges Blindeforbund would remain a Great Fundraising Organization.

Key Takeaways

Money is an emotional topic, and people can often become paralyzed when it comes to investment and risk, especially if they are expected to make decisions without adequate data. Part of your job as a fundraising director is to help your board and senior leadership overcome any emotional barriers to fundraising investment. This means being proactive in building out the decision-making capacity of these key stakeholders, as well as providing the forward-looking data that the leadership needs to make these decisions.

There are several tools and tips that can help you. Predictive KPIs are key performance indicators that look ahead, not back, and that stack up in a pyramid to the formula at the top: LTV divided by CPA. Scenario-based budgeting is also an excellent tool to create pace in an organization and inspire confidence and trust among the board and senior leadership regarding the fundraising team's capabilities.

An organization that faces forward is, by nature, operating in a space of uncertainty. Within that uncertainty, you can create trust by developing a track record of setting targets and meeting them, as well as demonstrating adaptability and learning as the information and results change.

Chapter 11

Leadership Decisions

In 2021, a number of successful organizations that we worked with approached me to understand how they could accelerate their whole organization alongside fundraising. By now, it had become abundantly clear that the fundraising department could not succeed without the buy-in of the rest of the organization. We knew the key to achieving this buy-in was leadership, but we needed further insights into how leadership could generate that alignment.

So I went back over our data to try to understand how an organization accelerates alongside fundraising. I found that, from the very first great fundraising research we commissioned from Professor Sargeant and Shang, it was clear that a critical component for success was what they called level 5 leadership.

Level 5 leadership, as identified by Professors Sargeant and Shang, is the phenomenon first discovered by Jim Collins in his book *Good to Great: Why Some Companies Make the Leap . . . and Others Don't*. Level 5 is defined as leadership with tremendous professional will combined with strong personal humility. The fundraising leaders of *all* Great Fundraising Organizations exhibited this level 5 leadership, which is what enabled their organizations to grow into their success.

Based on this insight, I conducted my own research. I contacted the leaders of numerous Great Fundraising Organizations and executed in-depth interviews to understand:

- What are the detailed characteristics of level 5 leadership?
- How do you develop level 5 leadership on an organizational basis?

The people I reached out to were all fundraising directors, as my research was, of course, focused on fundraising success. But every single fundraising director I contacted – all of whom were incredible leaders in their own right – wanted to bring their CEOs into the interview and conversation. They said, *I couldn't have done it without the chief executive.*

It turns out that the first task of a great fundraising director was to form a team with their CEO. It is exactly what we saw with Feenix in Chapter 2: Nyasha Njela, the fundraising director, and Leana de Beer, the CEO, consciously created a leadership coupling that helped them effectively radiate change throughout the organization. It was the same leadership coupling that we saw again and again across the Great Fundraising Organizations: fundraising directors and CEOs working hand in hand, operating in a space of level 5 leadership, to transform their nonprofits. The CEOs agreed to clear the way so fundraising could succeed; in turn, the fundraising directors agreed to deliver on the promised fundraising income.

Once they formed this team, both CEO and fundraising director had to bring the rest of the senior leadership team and the board into the level 5 leadership space for their endeavor to succeed. The uncomfortable truth is that this was not always easy. Often, it required a change in personnel – not everyone, but there were normally one or two people who had to move on to fulfill another organization's purpose. Both the CEO and the fundraising director did not waver in the face of these changes. They executed without compromise.

I loved this set of interviews because it was the first time I got to work at the macro level. Every leader I spoke to, fundraising directors and CEOs alike, were natural level 5 leaders. The research let us ask (1) what precisely does that mean and (2) how does one take what is intuitive to oneself and make it a structural and cultural part of an organization? It was a brilliant exercise. Our original research had said that the difference between great fundraising leaders and the rest was not so much what they did but how they thought. This is precisely what we found. These leaders displayed tremendous will with deep personal humility, characteristics that shaped how they thought and therefore how they approached problems and led their companies.

In my experience, the leaders of Great Fundraising Organizations are every bit as uncompromising as leaders in the private sector. They are able to make equally tough, and often controversial, decisions, and they are able to drive dramatic change through an organization despite resistance. But the nature of their conviction and resilience differs from their counterparts in the private sector. It is rooted in the belief in their organization's purpose.

Deep down, these leaders believe that the purpose of an organization is more important than anything. All decisions in the Great Fundraising Organization were not derived from the individual or any desire to come across as impressive or powerful but from a belief in the nonprofit's mission. This profound belief was present in every leader I interviewed. It was humbling to see how important it was to them.

For your organization to accelerate alongside fundraising and your nonprofit to succeed as a Great Fundraising Organization, level 5 leadership is vital. Working from a space of tremendous will and personal humility allows leadership to make three key decisions without compromise to kickstart growth. Without level 5 leadership, however, organizations find themselves stalled due to a deep-rooted fear: the fear of criticism.

Hierarchy of Purpose

The three key decisions leadership needs to make to trigger the Red Dot and ensure the whole organization is accelerating alongside fundraising are:

- Be as good at meeting the needs of your donors as you are at meeting the needs of your service users.
- Prioritize the optimization of fundraising investment as appropriate.
- Find the right communication hierarchy that delivers internal alignment and external differentiation, and commit to it.

None of these will be a surprise to you, as they are the three key issues and solutions we have been discussing throughout this book. Meeting the needs of your donors addresses the cultural conflict (Chapter 1) and speaks to the culture block of the Trifecta (Chapter 6). Prioritizing fundraising investment addresses the investment conflict (Chapter 1) and fulfills the investment block of the Trifecta (Chapter 5). Creating the right communications hierarchy that delivers on internal alignment and external differentiation refers to the new ambition block of the Trifecta (Chapters 3 and 4), which speaks to the communications conflict (Chapter 1).

If the leadership can execute on all three decisions, with the overarching goal of being the best at their two businesses within their nonprofit, then the organization will be able to trigger a Red Dot and then keep triggering a Red Dot to grow into a Great Fundraising Organization.

So where does level 5 leadership come into this? Why is it so vital?

Level 5 leadership solves for a problem in executing these three decisions. As we have discussed before, the fundraising team behaves more like a private-sector business within a charity because fundraising must earn its income. This means it needs pace. To achieve pace, it needs crisp decision-making: authoritative decisions that can be rolled out quickly and firmly to keep the organization moving. In simple terms, it needs an element of a decision-making hierarchy.

Now, traditional hierarchical structures do not work in nonprofits. Hierarchy based on positions and people's personalities is ineffective in the charity space; there is no place for them. People don't go work for a nonprofit to have a domineering boss shout at them.

Thus, we have a conundrum: you need a hierarchy of decision-making to drive pace as a Great Fundraising Organization, but the hierarchy of position and people will cause staff to leave. How do you solve for it?

The solution is clear in our dataset: it lies in level 5 leadership. Level 5 leaders are anchored in their organization's mission and purpose; it is their paramount driver of action. Successful organizations, therefore, created a hierarchy of purpose. They created a framework where purpose was the top anchor, dividing into the new ambition and theory of change for the two businesses of the nonprofit. This drove all subsidiary decisions because there was a defined and uncompromised point of reference against which to make all choices.

In terms of fundraising, once the new ambition was defined, it was entirely possible to push decision-making power far deeper into the organization because the parameters within which the team had the freedom to make decisions were pre-agreed. Once an organization has that, they can move at speed.

Different organizations used various terminologies for their hierarchy of purpose. Some went as far as to adopt the circles model of

Leadership Decisions

organizational development. Others had simple guidelines and buy-in. But they all created pace by adopting a simple cut-through line:

Purpose is boss.

In other words, decisions get fast when purpose is boss. This is what every Great Fundraising Organization, in their different ways, managed to achieve. By anchoring on the purpose as the reference point, they were able to create a decision-making hierarchy that helped execute the three key decisions to kickstart and sustain growth.

Fear of Criticism

This is a section of the book that will probably raise the hackles of a lot of people. I have hesitated about whether to be so direct about this, but we must tell uncomfortable truths, no matter the consequences.

Organizations that fail to achieve level 5 leadership fail because there is too much ego and fear combined in their key leaders or in the senior leadership group. If level 5 leadership is a combination of tremendous will with personal humility, then the combination of ego and fear is its direct opposite.

Why is this combination so damaging? It is because when an organization or leader is run by ego plus fear, then looking good becomes more important to them than anything else. Reputational management becomes their sole concern rather than achieving the nonprofit's purpose, and they are driven by an acute fear of criticism.

There are two sources of criticism for any nonprofit: internal and external. Internal criticism is criticism from the staff about the leadership, while external criticism is negative feedback from outside the organization and can range from complaints by donors to negative media coverage. When fear of criticism becomes a more powerful driver than "purpose is boss" for senior leadership, then an organization becomes paralyzed. They are incapable of making any decision due to fear of backlash. They retreat and derive comfort from indecision and compromise.

This connects back to what we talked about in Chapter 2, in the section "Shifting Mindsets: From Governance to Growth." Leadership has to decide if they see their prime role as managing an organization or solving a problem. If they decide it is managing an organization, then protecting against reputational damage becomes paramount. But if they decide it is solving a problem, then they must focus on solving the problem irrespective of the criticism that comes their way.

In those organizations that adopt a growth mindset and pave a path toward becoming a Great Fundraising Organization, any leader who operates with a combination of ego plus fear simply leaves. The environment is not conducive to their way of thinking, for in a Great Fundraising Organization, purpose is boss. But even if those ill-matched leaders leave and you solve for an individual fear of criticism, you can still be left with an institutional fear of criticism.

Let us be clear: there will always be some degree of an institutional fear regarding critique and backlash. Nobody in the world likes to be criticized. So how do you solve for this fear?

A level 5 leader accepts that their organization's purpose mandates that they tell uncomfortable truths. It is not a choice. Therefore, they accept that if they have taken on the responsibility of speaking up about an uncomfortable truth, some form of criticism is inevitable. They cease to put their energy into avoiding criticism. Instead, they put their focus – and, if needed, their resources – into preplanning and sharpening their response to any criticism. This way, they can proceed with confidence that when the inevitable criticism does come, they can proceed with integrity and the knowledge that their response will produce a positive result.

This is what we found in the set of interviews I conducted with the great fundraising leaders and their CEOs. In almost every interview, the response to criticism was the same: *We are able to prepare for criticism by accepting that purpose is boss. It is our job to work toward our purpose, no matter what uncomfortable truths it reveals, and if we don't do it, we will be failing our service users.*

This means that a Great Fundraising Organization spends time aligning across the organization for their purpose, new ambition, and theory of change. But once they have settled on those reference points, the leadership gives the staff the power to go out and speak these truths with integrity but without compromise. They make it clear: the leadership has the team's back.

Illustration: The RNLI, United Kingdom

One of the best examples of level 5 leadership being a structural and cultural part of an organization and shaping its response to criticism is the RNLI. Most of the fundraisers reading this book will recognize this story because it rocketed around the world online.

In 2021, there was a lot of media coverage in the United Kingdom about what some people termed as "migrants." Many of these migrants were asylum seekers or refugees crossing the English Channel from France to England in small, unstable boats. It was a tragic news story; there were a lot of desperate people and far too many deaths. The English Channel is a very dangerous stretch of water to be crossing when you have an overcrowded, inflatable boat. The number of people dying on those crossings was heartbreaking.

The RNLI, of course, had lifeboat stations along the south coast of England because it was a busy shipping lane. Any time one of these unstable boats got into trouble, the RNLI would send out a

---

Great Fundraising Organizations

lifeboat to save the lives of the people onboard and, if necessary, bring them to the shore. It happened on a regular basis.

At that time, certain segments of the British population had a bad reaction to these boats. A politician heavily criticized the RNLI for saving these desperate people who were trying to get into the country. This galvanized a British newspaper – which had a particular distaste for immigration and migrants – into action. On a Sunday, they dropped a cover story that essentially said, "The RNLI is facilitating illegal immigration. You should stop donating to them."

Now, the RNLI had anticipated this would happen. They may not have known about the news story dropping on a Sunday, but they expected backlash for the work they were doing, and they had their response prepared. Their purpose was very clear: "Save lives at sea." Their new ambition, as we saw in Chapter 9, was "To Save Every One." Both of these anchors were crystal clear in their guidance: if someone was in danger in the water, the RNLI had a duty to save them.

So the organization came out swinging. That Sunday, the RNLI drafted an immediate social media response that doubled down on their purpose. The RNLI didn't mince words. Yes, they rescue people in the English Channel. Yes, they would continue to do it. Their only sadness was they could not save everyone yet.

Posted that Sunday, they put out extensive communications that communicated their pride in the work they were doing. Volunteer crew members sent in stories about people they had rescued in the English Channel. They recorded videos talking about how the children they were saving reminded them of their own children. The RNLI put their response to the article on the front

(continued)

(continued)

page of their website. They parried every criticism by pulling the conversation back to the organization's purpose and reiterating their commitment to it. Their ambition wasn't "To save a particular kind of person." It was to "To Save Every One." They meant it.

I cannot describe how emotional this was for everyone involved, internally and externally, to see a charity publicly declare that their purpose was more important than any criticism they could receive. It was heartwarming, inspiring, humble, tragic – all at the same time.

And the fundraising outcome of all this? A very small number of people, no more than 100, chose to stop making their monthly donations to the RNLI. Total donation income increased by 71% over this period in response to the RNLI's campaign, replacing those few lost donors many, many times over.

Key Takeaways

The fear of criticism is often dressed up as a fear of damaging the reputation of an organization and thus its growth. *If we are criticized*, people say, *our revenue and income will drop*. While it is true that catastrophic reputational damage can hurt a nonprofit's income, more often than not, long-term purpose transcends any short-term criticism.

When you allow yourself to be run by fear, you are allowing yourself to be run by emotion, not data. As a leader, a fear of criticism can paralyze you from making meaningful change in your organization and working toward growth and the Red Dot.

Level 5 leaders do not focus on eradicating criticism but on developing their response to it. They anticipate what might be said and prepare a robust reply that allows them to move forward with integrity. These leaders work with tremendous will and personal humility and are driven by their organization's purpose. This is the anchor that guides them. The nonprofit's purpose, they believe, transcends everything, and it forms the cornerstone for their decision-making and their response to critique. Level 5 leaders can be strong and uncompromising when the occasion calls for it – not because they are driven by ego or a desire to be right but because furthering the organization's purpose is dearly important to them.

In Great Fundraising Organizations where level 5 leadership is a structural and cultural reality, the whole organization creates pace and scale through a hierarchy of purpose. This hierarchy places the organization's purpose as the key reference point for all decisions, which allows the organization, particularly the fundraising team, to move at pace and operate at a speed that facilitates sustainable growth.

If you are looking to become a Great Fundraising Organization, focus on level 5 leadership. Then team up with your CEO, and work together to bring the board and the rest of the senior leadership team into a level 5 leadership space. Once you do, you will have set your organization up for success. And if you and your leadership team are already level 5 leaders, then great! Crack on as fast as you can.

Chapter 12

How to Get Going

There are many reasons why an organization may need to grow their fundraising revenue. Some are looking to increase their impact. Others have expanded the range of problems they want to address. One common reason we have encountered is because the core problem the nonprofit is addressing has grown – which means the nonprofit must expand to tackle it.

This was the case with the Macular Society in the United Kingdom. Macular disease, which causes loss in the central field of vision and is currently incurable, is not exclusively a disease of old age. However, the majority of its incidence tends to be age related. As the aging population in the United Kingdom increased, so did the number of people living with macular disease in all forms – from life-changing to life-limiting to blindness.

I am not sure how Cathy Yelf, the CEO of the Macular Society, heard about our research on the Great Fundraising Organizations, but once she did, she set about implementing our insights to transform her nonprofit. She began with her board. Luckily, her board were natural level 5 leaders, and they grasped the importance of what she was trying to do. They backed her all the way.

Next, Cathy realized the Macular Society needed a level 5 leader in the fundraising department. She advertised for the post with a prerequisite that the charity would be growing over the next decade with our Great Fundraising Organization research as the basis of their strategy, and any applicant must buy in to this vision. This is how they found Emma Malcolm, who went on to become their director of fundraising.

Three months before Emma officially joined as director, she flew out to Scotland with the rest of the Macular Society board and team to attend a masterclass at our Loch Ness center. This was a masterclass on the Great Fundraising Organizations combined with seminars to find the Macular Society's new ambition and put their Trifecta in place.

The Macular Society found their new ambition in "Beat macular disease." It was short and to the point, but it featured a crucial word, "beat," which brought together the desire for people with macular disease to overcome it, as well as the desire of researchers to eventually find a cure for it or a way to prevent it. The board then spent a seminar finding the optimum level of investment and creating an investment plan. The cultural change had already begun: the board and senior leadership were aligned in their cultural shift and poised to roll it out across the organization. By the end of the multiday masterclass at Loch Ness, the Macular Society's Trifecta was almost in place.

But the breakthrough moment for the Macular Society occurred in the emotional space. For the longest time, while trying to shape their new ambition, the Macular Society were unsure about who their donors were and what their needs could be. Initially, there was a reluctance to fundraise from people with macular disease or from their family and friends. Thus, the organization pondered an interesting problem: how on earth do you raise money from people who are not affected by macular disease for the people who are?

They couldn't find any answers. Then a board member told the story of how he had had no experience of macular disease and believed it to be a disease of old age – until his son was diagnosed with it at six years old. It was a pivotal moment because it helped the organization realize that every senior leadership or board member in the room either had experience with macular disease or they knew someone affected by it. Turns out, the people with the biggest need to give to their organization were the people with macular disease or their family or friends. Their service users and their donors were the same.

This was, of course, a limitation of their fundraising market. But once they accepted this limitation, they realized it wasn't so narrowing – the fundraising market was still large. And just because the service user and the donor were the same person, it didn't mean they had the same needs.

As a service user, those with macular disease accepted that they would always have the illness and were looking for ways to work with the charity to best manage it during their lifetime so they could live an improved life. As a donor, those with macular disease were determined to pass on their life experience to future generations so the next generation wouldn't have to live with the disease.

This circles back to what we talked about in Chapter 1: your two businesses will always be different, even when they share the same client. The donor and the service user for the Macular Society were the same person, but they had different needs that had to be met in different ways.

After the masterclass, the Macular Society implemented their learnings with remarkable thoroughness. With the Trifecta now in place, the senior leadership rebuilt the Macular Society with the structural building blocks for a Great Fundraising Organization that we saw in Chapter 6, which they backed up with memes (also covered in Chapter 6). The result? Over a five-year period, their income increased by 131%, which was almost two and a half times what they were raising before. They are still growing.

Macular Society

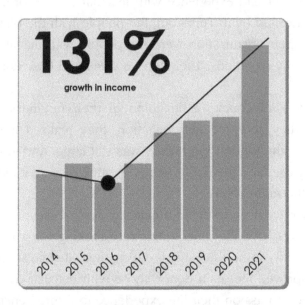

Figure 12.1 Macular Society growth chart.
Source: Revolutionise International Limited 2024.

The Macular Society would never have achieved these results if they hadn't worked in the emotional space. Except for total market universe – which is everyone in your market – the biggest roadblocks for fundraising are emotional. There is no way around these road-blocks without compromising. You must simply go *through* them.

To put it another way, the organizations that flatline have three distinct behaviors that are easily identifiable, each of which is the opposite of the Trifecta:

- They try to solve cultural problems with structural solutions (i.e. constant restructures without addressing core cultural issues).

- They try and solve emotional problems with logical solutions (i.e. adding more and more detail to their communications rather than approaching and working on the problem in an emotional space).

- They consistently have short-term, financial knee-jerk responses to more deep-rooted and structural financial issues, such as lack of growth.

A brilliant summary of all three of these behaviors would be they are trying to solve emotional problems with logical solutions. Simple as that.

Everything my 55 years of life have taught me proves that you cannot solve emotional problems by thinking about them. You can only solve emotional problems by *acting* and proving to yourself that you are good enough and can succeed. Action and self-evidencing success are what build belief.

I am constantly amazed by the number of people who are reticent about working in an emotional space when it comes to fundraising growth, to the point of objecting to it, and who then, five years later, are immensely proud of their work and claim they were onboard from the beginning. It's a constant source of wonder and amusement.

This is not to say, of course, that there are no logical aspects to creating a Great Fundraising Organization. Growth is based on data, analysis, predictive KPIs, and clear behavioral analyses of your donor base and their needs. But working in an emotional space and striving for emotional excellence are paramount. I remember talking to Rasmus Kjeldahl, the CEO of Børns Vilkår, about this. He is a fairly logical and analytical man himself, and he is well-networked in the corporate and nonprofit spaces in Copenhagen. He told me that he could tell within 12 minutes which organizations were going to succeed in fundraising and which weren't. He said, "I can tell immediately the ones who have been to the emotional space and are comfortable working in it compared to the ones who aren't. The ones who aren't will not make it."

If you are looking to grow your fundraising for your nonprofit, learn *how* to do it by *doing* it. Except for the market universe, all the biggest roadblocks are emotional. Your only way past them is through them.

Eight Steps to Success

People are driven by two elements: dreams and fears. Dreams are why people do things; fears are why people don't. If you want to motivate your organization so that you can execute to become a Great Fundraising Organization, the trick is to make the dream bigger than the fear.

This involves acknowledging, at the onset, that creating a Great Fundraising Organization depends on aligning your people rather than building your plan. This doesn't mean that plans are not important. You need plans to create budgets and move forward, but if you believe that planning – and therefore guaranteeing an outcome – is how you overcome fear, then your nonprofit will be routed to failure. Plans are not fixed, immovable roads. I have never seen a plan go from A to Z without changing; they are not the anchor to which you can attach your fundraising growth. Don't keep waiting for the "perfect plan."

Instead, focus on your people. They are the key determinant of your success, as well as the main hurdle to it. In simple terms, it's a people thing. So, how do you make the dream bigger than the fear in your organization so that the people you work with are aligned and motivated? You focus on the nonprofit's purpose. Senior leadership must find a way to make the dream of fulfilling the organization's purpose bigger more critical than the fear of failing or of criticism.

Think of it like the JFK strategy. The JFK government decided to go to the moon and set themselves a deadline: 1969. Then they fired up the people and rewrote the plan goodness knows how many times just so that they could meet that deadline. As long as the people were focused, inspired, and aligned, they could manage anything thrown at them.

Here are the eight steps to making the dream of an organization's purpose bigger than the fear of failing. They incorporate the learnings of this book into a simple, step-by-step process you can implement as the director of fundraising from the moment you turn the last page of this book. Remember, the key to this is action: you can only build belief in your organization by consistent execution. Don't get bogged down by the hope for a perfect plan. Act. It will make all the difference.

Build Your Troupe

The first step is to get the right people on board with your plan. This means ensuring that the CEO supports you in your endeavor to build a Great Fundraising Organization and that you have the support of the board and the senior leadership. Not everyone on the board or senior leadership will back you, but this is okay – you simply need a decision-making majority. In essence, at this step, you are seeking to build a level 5 leadership team that can lead the organization toward becoming a Great Fundraising Organization.

See: Chapters 11 and 2.

Train Your Leadership

Once you have your level 5 leadership team in place, begin training them on the fundamentals of fundraising and running a fundraising business. A Great Fundraising Organization is two businesses in one: most of your board and senior leadership will be excellent at the business that meets the needs of your service users, but they will have very little understanding of how fundraising needs to function to succeed and meet the needs of your donors. Teaching them the fundamentals will go a long way in helping them measure fundraising process, success, and investment.

See: Chapter 1.

Create a New Ambition

Once the leadership is on board and trained, it is time to build out your Trifecta. Start with your new ambition. Inspire the entire organization through the process of agreeing to your 5- or 10-year goal. Once you have that goal, don't compromise on it for as long as it takes to achieve it.

Creating your new ambition requires having a nuanced understanding of your donor and their needs. It also means working in an emotional space. We call this the "Go to Church" technique, where – after the organization has done the logical analyses of donor segments, needs, and services – you sit together as an organization in an emotional space and share stories. It reminds everyone of why they are here and usually leads to a breakthrough that aligns the organization and unlocks the framing of the new ambition.

See: Chapters 3, 4, 7, and 8.

Embed the Culture

Once you have your new ambition, you can roll out the second block of the Trifecta: the culture. This can be done in two ways: through systematic building blocks or memes. It must be reinforced consistently through training, especially for new recruits joining the organization.

The emotional space is equally important when it comes to culture. You will have sat down and shared stories to create your new ambition, but it is vital that you keep accessing this emotional space regularly to ensure culture stays aligned.

See: Chapters 6 and 7.

Data

Data overcomes fear, so ensure you collect data on the financial and fundraising history of your organization to get buy-in from your board and senior leadership regarding your financial plan. Make sure you do your testing and your benchmarking against other organizations. A small note on benchmarking: be prepared to look internationally. If you are working with a very specific cause in one country, your closest benchmark might be the same cause in a different country rather than a different cause in your country.

See: Chapter 5.

Create an Investment Plan

Using the data, create an investment plan that can help you roll out your new ambition, as well as create the tools you need to manage the investment plan. By this, we mean the predictive KPIs, scenario-based budgeting and modeling, testing, etc.

See: Chapter 10.

Line Up and Go

Once you have the Trifecta in place and the whole organization on board, it is time to line up and go. As we mentioned in the Introduction, the first day of a new fundraising strategy can feel like the organization is relaunching itself. It is exciting and empowering in equal measure – positive change feels right around the corner.

A good tip to ensure your relaunch is a success is to get your senior leadership to be the public face of the new fundraising strategy. Several years ago, Maree Daniels, the executive manager at RSPCA Western Australia, convinced her chair, CEO, and chief inspector to front the relaunch – i.e. they did all the press interviews and external communications – while she stayed behind the scenes keeping the campaign moving and, more importantly, managing the relationships with new donors. The new strategy was a resounding success: about 20,000 people (1% of the entire state population) made their first gift to RSPCA Western Australia's relaunch campaign.

Keep Going

Once you have launched your new fundraising strategy, your task is to keep going until you achieve your goal. As always, this is simple but not easy. At the start of a new strategy, the energy is always high. As you continue, however, and people become busier and less focused, it is natural for the energy to drop. Your job as a fundraising leader is to raise those energy levels back up so your organization can keep moving at pace.

Why is this so important? When people are tired and drained, they resort to compromise, and compromise affects the success of your Red Dot. When you find your organization is flagging, get back into the emotional space and reconnect with the nonprofit's purpose. Go back to your "why." Use your troupe – i.e. the other like-minded people in the organization at the top leadership – to help you recenter the organization and inspire the staff to keep going.

These are the eight ways in which you, as fundraising director, can execute what you have learned in this book in a streamlined manner to help your organization become a Great Fundraising Organization.

That said, a vital characteristic of a Great Fundraising Organization is they keep triggering Red Dots repeatedly. Which brings us to:

Bonus: Do it All Again

When you sense a surge is achieved and you are nearing the end of what you can accomplish with your new ambition, it is time to start another one.

If you look back over the careers of great fundraising leaders, the research shows that they drove growth through a series of surges. This means that, intuitively, they recognized that when growth flat-lined, it was because the organization had become confused and tired, and so they stepped back to create clarity and a new point of purpose that the organization could rally around. In other words, they began the process of triggering a new Red Dot.

Iain McAndrew at CHAS achieved massive success with their new ambition. Just last month, he got in touch with me and asked, "Can we spend half a day with the leadership team to answer the question, 'What's next?'" The answer essentially boiled down to three things:

- Raise the bar (i.e. increase the ambition again)
- Line up everyone behind it (get alignment)
- Go really fast

This is what you must do too. When your organization has exhausted its Red Dot, turn around and do these eight points again.

The Key Takeaway

Since this is the last chapter, I am going to deviate from our chapter format. We don't need a summary for this chapter because it is, after all, the summary of the chapters that came before it. Instead, I want to leave you with the key takeaway for this book, the number one learning that will help you implement these insights on a day-to-day level.

Dr. Iain MacRitchie had a long and spectacular career in corporate turnarounds and accelerations before leaving it behind eight years ago to self-fund and build a charity helping

(continued)

(continued)

care-experienced young people, MCR Pathways. He started this charity in Glasgow, Scotland, and scaled it throughout the United Kingdom. We are mates: he helps me with business, and I help him with purpose. It's a great symbiosis.

Iain often offers me simple nuggets regarding the behaviors that drive acceleration, which I absolutely love. One day, he told me about an initialism, RPD, which is a way of thinking and behaving that changes everything in the day-to-day. RPD stands for:

- Results
- Processes
- Deadline

To understand why RPD is so crucial, we will have to back up a little. Throughout this book, we have looked at big-picture growth. We have talked about level 5 leadership, the Trifecta, the transformational leadership that you need in the fundraising business to drive growth, the concept of "purpose in boss." But what in the detail makes organizational change happen in the day-to-day?

The answer is RPD. RPD is how you take the big picture and bring it down to what the fundraiser has to do in the everyday to create the organizational shift from a nonprofit that stagnates or flatlines to a Great Fundraising Organization.

It is easy enough to understand the components of RPD. "Results" refers to the end result you are trying to achieve. "Deadline" is the date by which you plan to achieve it. "Process" is how you plan to get from where you are to that chosen result.

Great Fundraising Organizations

In the services business of a nonprofit, the most important element of RPD is the process. This is because the avoidance of error is everything for the services department. Good processes keep people safe; they protect vulnerable populations; they eliminate error. In the services departments, therefore, process must be thorough, and it has to be adhered to no matter what. Results and deadline, however – the other elements of RPD – can vary depending on the needs and demands of the process (i.e. they can be changed so that process can be adequately fulfilled).

In the fundraising business of a nonprofit, however, it is the opposite. Fundraising needs pace and momentum. You create this by spending a lot of time identifying the correct result you are seeking and the correct deadline for that result. Once that result and deadline are signed off on and the project is initiated, these two elements become immovable. They cannot be changed. The only element of RPD that is fluid is process.

If people are allowed to change either results or deadline when it comes to fundraising, then people will inevitably choose to change those two elements (they are easier to shift, after all), and everything will slow down. Fundraising depends on pace. It is the opposite of bureaucracy. Bureaucracy exists in the services department for a very good reason – it protects vulnerable service users – but it doesn't have any place in a fundraising business.

RPD is the detailed manifestation of everything we have covered in this book. What does it look like executed? Firstly, you have to define your results. How do you choose the correct result that fundraising should try to achieve? Ask yourself, *Does the project advance the organization toward its purpose?* If it does, check if it is on strategy about how you focus your resources.

(continued)

How to Get Going

(continued)

If the result you have put down neither advances you toward your purpose nor your strategy, then do not adopt it. But if it does move you closer to your purpose and strategy, then you need to quantify the result, define its contribution to your organization's purpose, and agree on its aims and objectives. Once you do that, you have a result you can lock in.

Next, you agree on and commit to a deadline. Only once results and deadline are in place do you then develop the best process – i.e. the best method and resources that you are going to apply to achieve your result and meet your deadline.

Invariably, your process will change. You will fall behind schedule, or a target won't work out. In organizations that stagnate, this is often the point at which they decide to change the deadline. Then, if they fall even further back, they move on to lowering the result. But in the Great Fundraising Organizations, neither result nor deadline can change. This means the only acceptable process becomes "whatever it takes."

This way of thinking clearly identifies the detailed behavior that is the day-to-day manifestation of two businesses, one mission. RPD is a three-letter initialism that the fundraising leader can use to change behavior on a daily basis to line it up with everything else this book has said about ambition, culture, and investment.

Illustration: All Stories in this Book

If you look at the examples and stories throughout this book, the path that each organization took toward transformation was different. They were different nonprofits with unique problems and strengths, which meant they had to focus on varying factors. But the end result for each one of them was focus and energy in their fundraising department, which created momentum.

In the example of Lutheran World Relief, it was simply the injection of speed that gave them immediate financial returns.

The fact that Feenix in South Africa prepped for the Trifecta and the building blocks of a Great Fundraising Organization before they even launched their first fundraising campaign meant their growth was explosive.

Organizations like Børns Vilkår and the Royal Flying Doctor Service have implemented this methodology repeatedly, relentlessly, keeping pace in their organizations.

What ties them all together? They accepted that being a high-quality, intellectually driven nonprofit for their service users could sit comfortably and successfully alongside a rapidly growing fundraising department. They accepted that they were two businesses in one – and they could, and should, be the best at both.

Conclusion

Fundraising is not begging. It is the organization's ability to earn their money by meeting the needs of their donors, and it is a vital, beautiful thing in its own right. The great fundraising leaders understood this, just as they understood that a Red Dot can be triggered when the behavior of an organization changes from tired and confused to energized and focused. Great Fundraising Organizations, during a surge, are able to anchor on their purpose and new ambition rather than on their internal structures and processes; they are able to work for and toward something that is greater than themselves.

This all begins with good leadership. As fundraising director, your task now is to drive change throughout your organization using the insights in this book. A good start is the eight practical steps we covered in Chapter 12. We've put together a simple graphic that summarizes the content of this book, which you can use as a visual reminder or an aid for others when building your troupe (Figure C.1). Down the line, it can also serve as a meme for your organization.

One last thing to bear in mind: just as you must travel down a practical, actionable journey to trigger your Red Dot (the eight steps described in Chapter 12), there is an emotional journey that your organization will undergo in the process of becoming a Great Fundraising Organization. We call this IED: inspiration, education, and design.

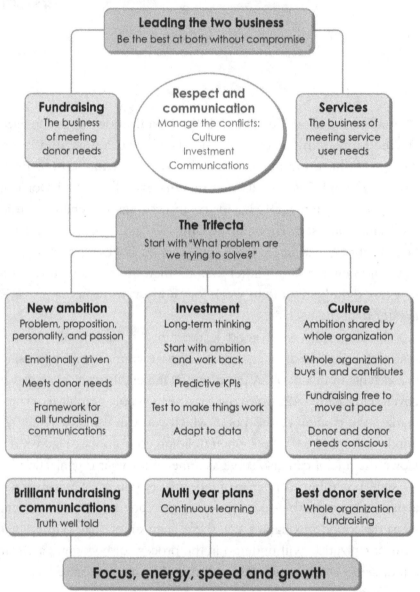

Purpose with precision
Differentiation and alignment

Leading the two business
Be the best at both without compromise

Fundraising
The business of meeting donor needs

Respect and communication
Manage the conflicts:
Culture
Investment
Communications

Services
The business of meeting service user needs

The Trifecta
Start with "What problem are we trying to solve?"

New ambition
Problem, proposition, personality, and passion

Emotionally driven

Meets donor needs

Framework for all fundraising communications

Investment
Long-term thinking

Start with ambition and work back

Predictive KPIs

Test to make things work

Adapt to data

Culture
Ambition shared by whole organization

Whole organization buys in and contributes

Fundraising free to move at pace

Donor and donor needs conscious

Brilliant fundraising communications
Truth well told

Multi year plans
Continuous learning

Best donor service
Whole organization fundraising

Focus, energy, speed and growth

Figure C.1 The master graphic.
Source: Revolutionise International Limited 2024.

Inspiration is about inspiring the rest of your organization regarding the insights and methodology in this book so that they believe it is possible. In other words, it's about convincing the rest of your senior leadership and other departments that this can work and earning their belief. We have found that the best way to gain belief is to spend time with people who have done it before, which is why we run detailed seminars for organizations to dive into our research and casework in greater detail: so that they recognize the evidence in front of them.

The second step, education, is about teaching the rest of your organization how to build a Great Fundraising Organization and trigger a Red Dot. Much of the methodology has been covered in this book, but we have stayed big picture in these chapters, which means there are multiple levels of detail in each topic that do not feature in this book and that could help your organization implement these insights.

There are two things to keep in mind about the education stage. First, the focus of the education must differ from organization to organization. Some nonprofits need to build their Trifecta from scratch; others need to create only the missing pieces. Make sure you are focusing on what your organization needs so that you build out a robust structural and cultural system of change. Second, the biggest hurdle to overcome at this stage is reluctance. You will be surprised at how many board members are convinced they don't need to be educated and who will bristle at the implication that they must learn something new. Others will simply not make time for it; getting a spot on the board meeting agenda for this type of learning can be one of the hardest things to do. This is an emotional barrier. Work through with the help of your troupe or experts.

Design, the last emotional stage, refers to the act of cocreating a Great Fundraising Organization with the other departments of the nonprofit. Creating the three elements of the Trifecta is not the responsibility of the fundraising department alone. It belongs to the whole organization, as we saw in Part 1. Thus, cocreating the Trifecta with colleagues from other departments is how you free yourself up to be the best at both your businesses. The majority of the blocks you will encounter during this process will be emotional; work through them with respect and communication.

I hope this book has offered you the answers you were looking for and that you feel revitalized and motivated to create change in your organization. You *can* break through the financial ceiling in fundraising and accelerate growth; there is a way that works. A great truism is everything in this book I have learned by spending time with and listening to the people who have done it. So, if you need help or you simply want to know more about our research and casework on the Great Fundraising Organizations, you can learn more through our website, Revolutionise.com.

Becoming a Great Fundraising Organization is a long game. You know this, of course; it is the key insight of this book. *Investing in professional fundraising is by far the best investment you'll ever make as long as you are prepared to think long-term*. But how do you stay motivated in the short-term in this long game?

The answer loops back to our Introduction: you remember the good you can achieve further in your career and you hold on to it. Then, as your career unfolds, pause every now and then to look at the world and see if it is a better place because of the effort you've poured in.

I had my moment of realization on a flight from Addis Ababa in Ethiopia to Vienna in Austria. I had just completed a seminar series in Addis Ababa and was spending my time in the air mulling over what an experience it was working there. I realized that in the early 1990s, when I began as a volunteer fundraiser, there were three places we were sending money: South Africa, which was battling with apartheid and then the aftereffects of apartheid; Ethiopia, which was recovering from the dreadful famines of the 1980s; and Romania, which was just uncovering the horrors of Ceausescu legacy and the thousands of children abandoned in those awful orphanages. In the 1990s, these were the three main countries receiving aid from wealthier countries.

Today, the reality is different. Over the course of my career, I have trained more than 400 fundraisers in South Africa, Ethiopia, and Romania who are now professionalizing due to the state of their expanded economies, nonprofit sector, and own donor populations. Their sheer amount of raw talent, genuine purpose, and drive consistently blow me away; they are not bogged down by institutional fear or bureaucracy that has paralyzed so many organizations in the West. Their fundraising entrepreneurship is alive and well – and it is inspiring. The credit for what they have built goes to them, but on that plane ride, I felt profound pride that I could have played some small part in their journeys. I thought to myself, *Wow, it feels like it's been a long time doing this – but boy, has the world remarkably changed.*

I wish the same realization for you. It does take a long time to do great things. But the one way to make the ending of these stories come faster is to go very, very fast right from the beginning. So, please, begin now.

Acknowledgments

There are many people at charities and nonprofits that have contributed to this book. Whether you are a client, have volunteered for research projects, allowed us to interview you, attended one of Revolutionise's seminars, or simply taken the research and run with it, thank you all for your commitment to a better world and to this study. I would like to single out Jayne George of the RNLI and previously Guide Dogs here in the United Kingdom. Jayne's willingness to take calculated risks, pilot new idea after new idea, and share widely has been pivotal both to those she serves and to our development. Jayne is a level 5 leader through and through.

Professors Adrian Sargeant and Jen Shang and their team at the Institute for Sustainable Philanthropy, notably Harriet Day and Dr. Kathryn Edworthy, have independently and diligently completed all the research briefs that are the backbone of Great Fundraising. They have come back time and time again with infinite patience and attention to detail and have stuck with us through times good and bad. The amount of money raised demonstrates that research is essential and effective, and investment in it is one of the best things we can do.

All any of us do is stand on the shoulders of giants, and that is all I have done for this book – learn from the best and summarize patterns in behaviors that create fundraising growth. I have been privileged to spend time, a great deal of it, with many of the best fundraising leaders, CEOs, and volunteer board members around the world. I particularly need to pay tribute to Ken Burnett and Giles Pegram, CBE. Both were very busy people when they stumbled upon me as an angry, frustrated, and unwell young man. They were generous in their time beyond the expectation of any reasonable person and helped me realize what is possible with dedication and diligence. They taught me a huge amount about fundraising and, more importantly, about the donors – those people that give so much. Richard "Haggis" Turner introduced me to this profession and has been fundraising with me in one way or another since the 1980s.

The team of consultants at Revolutionise keep me inspired always. Every one of them is a successful practitioner in their own right, and they too have been generous in sharing experience and detail to which I am not always privy, with our ongoing research and with their clients. Pat Dade at Cultural Dynamics deserves a special mention for all his work on values, which is so insightful. Kathy, Warren, Jay, and the team at Robejohn in Melbourne were courageous early adopters and, perhaps more importantly, persistors.

Tashan Mehta will edit this after I write it and will try to take it out. It's here, so you can see I didn't let her. Tashan, of Hal Clifford Associates, is my professional cowriter for this book and has brought insight, intelligence, drive, and, I must say, a truly joyful personality to this project, helping me distill thousands of pages into something of readable length with some structure. I've loved every minute of working with her.

The team at Wiley deserve super thanks – firstly for being bold enough to take this project on and for their sheer professionalism in guiding me through it all.

Jeff C. and the others in the fellowship will know that without 10 years of sobriety, this whole thing would not have happened.

My little family, Malene and Tor, have been dragged here, there, and everywhere as we carry out research and serve clients. They have put up with my moods and odd working hours. Malene is wonderful at challenging me on every specific point of fundraising, and Tor makes me laugh when I am down and makes me very, very proud all the time.

The biggest acknowledgment of all goes to all those people routinely categorized as "donors." All those men, women, and nonbinary people, all the mums, dads, daughters, sons, grannies, and grandads who have love in their souls and are prepared to act on it. Each has their own unique life story, and without them, professional fundraising would not exist, nonprofits would be a pipe dream, and the world would be a far, far poorer place.

Index

C

Cancer Research United
    Kingdom, 87
  ambition, 89
Capital value, impact, 210
Cascading effect, 69–70
Centre for Creative Education
    (CCE), 75–76
Charity
  growth, 233–234
  long-term perspective, 107
  space, attitude, 126
Charity Air Ambulance,
    purpose/funding
    ambition (search), 105
Child poverty, levels
    (increase), 200
Children's Hospices Across
    Scotland (CHAS),
    106, 200, 243
  fundraising issues, 77–80
  growth chart, 80f
  individual giving income,
    increase, 79
  rebranding, 78
Children/youth charities, 173f
Chinchen, Rosie, 154, 155
Christian Blind
    Mission (CBM)
  donors, conversion, 21
  interaction, human
    contact, 22

Claire House Children's
    Hospice, 159–162
  growth chart, 161f
Clients, successes/failures
    (importance), 3–4
Collins, Jim, 221
Communications
  conflict, 30, 35–37, 52
    Great Fundraising
      Organizations
      management, 41
  hierarchy, 70–72, 71f
Compound growth, 107–108
  marginal developments,
    basis, 108f
Conflict, elimination
    (avoidance), 37–38
Connection (donation
    reason), 166
Consensus-seeking
    compromise, 128
Cooperation, need, 176
Cost per acquisition
    (CPA), 209, 220
  improvement, 212, 213
  optimization, 213
COVID-19 pandemic
  damage, 216
  impact, 123–124, 185
Craig, David, 106
Creative connection,
    importance, 76

260

Index